Laughing Out Loud While Dying Inside

One Cop's Journey Through Trauma

by

Lt. Fred Jones (Ret)

COLEMAN JONES
PRESS

Published in West Palm Beach, FL, by Coleman Jones Press

www.ColemanJonesPress.com

ISBN:

Dedication

This book is dedicated to the men and women of law enforcement and their friends and family.

Acknowledge

While expressing my gratitude, I must first acknowledge my wife's unwavering support, a beacon of strength throughout the years. Her steadfast presence during the countless nights, offering solace and patience after the rigors of each shift, has been my sanctuary.

Furthermore, I appreciate Randy Friedman and Linda Webb, visionaries behind the RITE Academy. Through their pioneering work in emotional intelligence, I first encountered profound insights into my emotional landscape. Their guidance equipped me with invaluable tools for navigating and mastering the intricate realm of emotions.

Their mentorship continues to illuminate a path for public safety professionals, not merely to endure but to forge a robust foundation of self-mastery and emotional regulation. Their contributions are a compass, guiding us toward resilience and excellence in our noble pursuits.

Introduction

It's not by chance you picked up this book. Although you and I may have never met, if you're on the front lines of law enforcement, I have a good idea why you're here. You see, I was in Law Enforcement for 26 years. I retired in August 2023, but have held many positions during my career, including Road Patrol Deputy, Hostage Negotiator, Crisis Intervention Coordinator, Lieutenant and Public Information Officer, I've worked in various units along the way, including Investigations, School Resource, and DARE, to name just a few.

I have seen more than my fair share of evil and injustice and have lived through more trauma than I care to share. There have been moments when I thought I wouldn't make it. There were days when I knew my most significant accomplishment would be simply getting out of bed. You've probably had days like that, but kept your feelings to yourself because you knew deep down no one could possibly understand what you were going through.

If you're anything like me or so many of the friends and colleagues I've lost along the way to suicide, you may have thought about just ending it all. If you can relate to this, know you're not alone. I've been there, and I understand where you are. Not only have I been there, but I found my way out of the darkness and so can you. If you're reading this, you know I didn't die. I made it out and learned a few things I'd like to share with you about this journey we're on as humans behind the badge.

My name is Lt. Frederick 'Fred' Jones. I am a nationally-certified Emotional Intelligence Trainer and Designated

Subject Matter expert. When I first learned about Emotional Intelligence, I became so impressed with the subject that I took a deep dive and applied it to my everyday life. I was invited to participate in developing a curriculum with law enforcement and mental health professionals around Florida called Mental Health Wellness for Law Enforcement Officers, so I know the power of it and what it can do for your life.

Not long after donning the uniform, I realized the weight it carried—each day brought new challenges and new horrors to witness. While I stood firm in the face of danger, the toll it took on my soul was undeniable.

The nights were the hardest. I was alone with my thoughts and haunted by the faces of those I couldn't save. I drowned my sorrows in alcohol, seeking solace in the numbness it brought. But no amount of liquor could silence the demons that waited and whispered in the shadows.

It wasn't until I hit rock bottom that I realized I needed help. Therapy became my lifeline; a safe harbor in the storm. Through tears and laughter, I began to unpack the trauma that had been weighing me down for so long. With each session I felt a little lighter and more mentally accessible.

But therapy was only part of the equation. I had to confront my own emotions to acknowledge the pain and anger that simmered beneath the surface. It was a journey of self-discovery that forced me to face the parts of myself I'd long ignored.

I felt a renewed sense of purpose as I began to heal. I knew that I couldn't undo the past, couldn't erase the pain I'd experienced. But perhaps my journey could act as a lighthouse for others struggling in the darkness.

Armed with my newfound knowledge of emotional intelligence, I set out to make a difference. I collaborated with mental health professionals and other law enforcement personnel to develop programs aimed at supporting Florida law enforcement officers in their battles with trauma. Together, we created a community of support and a network of compassion where no one had to suffer in silence.

As I look back on my career, I see not just the hardships but also the triumphs. I see the lives I've touched and the hearts I've healed. Although the road has been long and arduous, I wouldn't trade it for anything.

To my fellow officers, I offer these words of encouragement: You are not alone. You are also resilient and capable of weathering any storm that comes your way.

To the families of law enforcement officers, Thank you for your steadfast support and unconditional love. You are the unsung heroes behind the badge, the silent strength that keeps us alive inside and out.

As for me, I may have retired my uniform, but I will never stop fighting for those who wear it. Ultimately, we are all just humans behind the badge, trying to make sense of a world gone mad.

In my 26-year journey as a law enforcement officer, I've witnessed the darkest sides of humanity. From responding to homicides and suicides to dealing with aggravated assaults and child abuse cases, each experience left its mark on my soul. Like many of you, I was engulfed in darkness, wondering if there was a way out.

But amidst the chaos and despair, there were moments of light. Moments that reminded me why I chose this path in the first place. Small moments and larger ones that showed me the impact I was making, even in the face of overwhelming adversity.

One such moment came when I delivered a TEDx talk titled, "Use of Voice; Not Force." This talk, which emphasized the power of Emotional Intelligence in law enforcement, resonated with thousands of viewers and became a staple in police academies across Florida. It was a testament to the importance of empathy and communication in our line of work.

But my journey didn't stop there. I continued to spread the message of Emotional Intelligence, training other law enforcement agencies and sharing my experiences on local and national television. I wasn't just preaching; I was living the principles I spoke about – principles that saved me from spiraling further into darkness.

As I share my story with you, I hope you'll find solace and guidance in my words. Whether you're here to heal yourself or someone you love, know there is a way out of the darkness. You are not alone, and your struggles are valid.

As you navigate the challenges of this career, remember to prioritize your emotional and mental health. It's okay to seek help and care for yourself, even as you dedicate your life to protecting and serving others. Today marks the beginning of your journey toward healing and resilience. Let's walk this path together.

"When I entered this profession, I was told my job was to protect and to serve, but no one told me that one day I would need to protect and serve myself, to take care of me."

-- Fred Jones

Chapter One

"I'm Tom Bodett. We'll leave the lights on for you."

In the field of law enforcement, where we often serve as the first line of defense against chaos and disorder, there exists a silent battle that many of us face within ourselves - the battle against trauma. It's reminiscent of that iconic Motel 6 TV commercial that ends with the comforting promise, "We'll leave the lights on." But what happens when your light goes out, as trauma sends us spiraling into darkness, with no one there to illuminate our path?

As a certified Emotional Intelligence trainer committed to fostering understanding between law enforcement and the community, I have spent the last seven years immersed in the intricate dynamics of human emotion within the profession. Through my journey of confronting and addressing trauma, I realize the critical importance of shining a light on this often-overlooked aspect of our lives.

It was during a period when I was not addressing my trauma when I found myself veering off course, succumbing to behaviors that were uncharacteristic of the person I've always strived to be. I experienced moments of quick temper, judgmental attitudes, and even bouts of apathy that seemed to envelop me without warning. These were not merely isolated incidents but rather consistent manifestations of the trauma that had taken root within me, rotting in the depths of my subconscious.

Unlike the sensationalized narratives that dominate social media, the pain inflicted by trauma is not always overt or physical. It can manifest in various forms, subtly yet profoundly influencing our thoughts, emotions, and behaviors. Through my experiences, I have come to understand that trauma, left unaddressed, has the power to negatively shape our actions and decisions, both as law enforcement officers and as individuals navigating the complexities of life.

My trauma manifested inwardly, casting a shadow over my daily life and robbing me of the clarity and purpose that once defined my existence. I found myself grappling with inexplicable tears, struggling to find the motivation to face each new day, and wrestling with a darkness that seemed to envelop me at every turn. It was as if I had lost sight of the light that once illuminated my path, leaving me adrift in a sea of uncertainty and despair.

But as I grappled with my inner demons, I came to realize that trauma thrives in the shadows, lurking in the recesses of our minds and waiting to ambush us when we least expect it. It feeds on our fears and insecurities, clouding our judgment and leading to unprofessionalism and poor decision-making.

It wasn't until I confronted my trauma head-on, when I discovered a source of strength and resilience that I never knew existed within me. By shining a light on the pain that had long been buried, I reclaimed control over my emotions and actions, empowering myself to navigate life's challenges with clarity and purpose. Much like taking a safe walk on a clear and illuminated path, rather than a dangerous walk on a dark and treacherous one.

My journey toward healing and self-discovery has taught me that trauma is not a sign of weakness but rather a testament to the resilience of the human spirit. It requires courage, vulnerability, and a willingness to confront the darkest corners of our minds. But it also holds the promise of redemption and renewal, allowing us to emerge from the shadows and step into the light of a brighter tomorrow.

As we reflect on the tumultuous year of 2020, dominated by the far-reaching effects of the COVID-19 pandemic, it becomes evident that the challenges faced by our nation extended far beyond the confines of a public health crisis. The unprecedented disruption to daily life and social and political upheaval created a perfect storm that tested the resilience of individuals and communities across the United States.

Amidst the chaos and uncertainty, I found myself drawing inward for solace and clarity. The year's events, from the ravages of the virus to social justice protests and counter-protests, seemed to be pulling the nation into a vortex of division and discord. As friends and acquaintances aligned themselves with various political factions and conspiracy theories, I witnessed the fracturing of relationships and the erosion of trust.

Navigating this tumultuous landscape reminded me of a profound truth: peace cannot coexist with anger. While some may profess to find solace in their rage, I discovered that true peace lies in the depths of silence within oneself. This journey led me to confront the internal noise that had long plagued me throughout my career in law enforcement.

My journey into the heart of my silence began amidst the din of prison environment, where I began my career as a corrections officer. The constant clamor of inmate grievances and complaints echoed through the facility's corridors, a relentless hum that followed me home at the end of each shift. The voices of those I supervised lingered in my mind and interrupted my inner peace.

Transitioning to a road patrol deputy role offered little respite from the constant noise that permeated my thoughts. The demands of the job, coupled with the weight of external pressures and expectations, only served to amplify the internal turmoil that stormed within me. It was a relentless assault on my senses, a ceaseless noise.

Yet, amidst the chaos, I began to discern a flicker of light amidst the darkness. It was a realization that true peace could only be found by confronting the internal demons that haunted me. I realized I had to find a way to silence the negative voices that clamored for attention within my mind. It was a journey of self-discovery and introspection, a path that led me to confront the trauma that had long resided dormant inside.

The weight of my role as a law enforcement officer stretched beyond the streets I patrolled. Eventually, it seeped into every aspect of my life, including the sanctuary of my home. The Communication Center (often likened to the conductor of an orchestra), directed the symphony of calls that dictated our actions on the road patrol. Dispatchers would guide us through a myriad of situations, from mundane lockouts to life-threatening emergencies like aggravated assaults or homicides. In the span of a twelve-hour shift, the multitude of calls created a constant background noise that echoed in my mind long after I had left the station. Each call for service followed me home, embedding itself in my thoughts and emotions. I grappled with doubt and uncertainty, second-guessing the decisions I made. In the quiet hours of the night, I struggled to find relief in sleep.

The darkness soon began to seep into my interactions with loved ones and colleagues, casting a pall over my behavior that was noted by those closest to me. My spouse and co-workers observed moments when my demeanor seemed out of character when the weight of my responsibilities manifested in ways that opposed the strength I sought to personify.

Amidst the darkness, I found hope—a solution to quiet the voices that plagued me. Through introspection and self-discovery, I began to confront the trauma that lay buried within me, reclaiming control over my emotions and actions. A journey of healing and redemption empowered me to face the darkness within and emerge more robust and resilient than before.

Question: Do you sometimes feel like you are walking in darkness? Has your spouse or co-worker ever said your behavior was out of character?

Chapter Two

News at Eleven

As the years passed, my law enforcement role extended beyond the confines of just road patrol. One of my pivotal positions was serving as a Public Information Officer, where my mornings commenced with the solemn task of reviewing arrest affidavits from the previous night. Within those documents lay the darkest corners of humanity, detailing crimes that ranged from simple battery to heinous acts of murder. The weight of these narratives bore down on me as I carefully redacted sensitive information before distributing it to the media.

One particular case would haunt my soul forever. It involved a call my Lieutenant and I responded to where a father (who was bitterly embroiled in a nasty divorce) had allegedly committed the unthinkable - drowning his toddler daughter in a bathtub. The gravity of the situation was palpable as I arrived at the scene, evidenced by the distressed looks of my fellow deputies and detectives. The death of a child at the hands of a parent is a horrible occurrence no one should ever have to bear witness to.

As I gathered my notes and prepared to face the glare of the media spotlight, I felt a weight upon my shoulders unlike anything I had experienced before. I was overwhelmed with grief as I approached reporters from local news stations - ABC, CBS, NBC, FOX - and smaller outlets from the Orlando market. Print media also descended upon the scene, eager to capture the grim details of this heart-wrenching tragedy.

In moments like these, I had become accustomed to navigating the delicate balance between transparency and discretion, ever-mindful of the ongoing investigation and the limited details that could be divulged. But the script was rewritten on this occasion just moments before I stepped before the cameras. Permission was granted to reveal the harrowing specifics of this unspeakable crime. A father had mercilessly taken the life of his own flesh and blood.

The weight of those words hung heavy in the air as I delivered the miserable details to a stunned audience. It was a moment that transcended the confines of law enforcement protocol, plunging me into despair and anguish. The trauma of reading the details of such a senseless act of violence, compounded by the responsibility of delivering the news to the public, left an indelible mark on my psyche.

In the aftermath of that fateful day, I found myself grappling with the profound implications of trauma within the law enforcement community. It was a wake-up call that prompted me to confront the silent struggles many of us face in the line of duty as we witness the darkest aspects of human nature. This realization fueled my passion for helping officers identify and address their trauma, empowering them to navigate the complexities of their profession with resilience and compassion.

As I stood before the cameras, poised to deliver the grim details of the tragedy that had unfolded before me, I found myself at a loss for words. Tears welled in my eyes as I lost the composure I had so meticulously crafted for the press. In that moment of vulnerability, I became acutely aware of the thousands of eyes fixed upon me. Fred, the human behind the badge.

Struggling to find my voice. I uttered some disjointed response; my words choked with tears. I remember stumbling through the interview. My mind was unable to remain calm and neutral in the wake of the tragedy I had just witnessed. It felt as though the life had been sucked out of me, leaving me momentarily stunned…while actively on camera.

In the aftermath of that experience, although I faced feelings of embarrassment and shame, I also found solace in the outpouring of support from my friends and colleagues. One friend's words echoed in my mind, reminding me that vulnerability is not a sign of weakness but a testament to our shared humanity. Through tears and trembling voice, I had laid bare the emotional toll of what it was like for the officers who see the darkest aspects of human nature. During that most awful moment, I revealed the human behind the badge.

That moment was a stark reminder of the traumas law enforcement officers are subjected to daily. Day in and day out, we confront the raw realities of human suffering, the pain and anguish of victims and perpetrators alike. Yet oftentimes, our trauma goes unacknowledged and untreated, festering beneath the surface and threatening to consume us from within.

Sometimes, it's not just about the heinous acts we have witnessed. Our wounds get intertwined with the calls we are sent to and only serve to aggravate them further. For example, I was a father. I was divorced. One of my greatest pains during the early years of my career was not being present enough for my daughter. It was during this moment when I was trying to balance my role as an officer and a father, constantly feeling like I was lacking in one or both. To this day, I'm still not sure if I cried on television because of all the things that I saw, and this was the straw that broke the camel's back, or if it was tapping into the perceived deficiencies that I had buried years before. Even so, I could never have imagined hurting my child. By taking a deep dive into Emotional Intelligence and regularly going to therapy, I picked up some tools to help me through my trauma.

Reflecting on this, I invite you to consider the following: When did you last feel you lost your composure in response to a call? Was something in your life (current or past) that triggered this situation?

Question: As an officer, what scene have you responded to that you can't seem to shake?

Chapter Three

"Is This Me?"

Law enforcement is a relentless profession that demands everything from those who serve within its ranks. The line between duty and personal sacrifice often gets blurred, and the weight of the badge can become unbearable if left unchecked.

Reflecting on my journey in law enforcement, I'm still haunted by particular scenes of tragedy and loss that have become imprinted upon my memory. How many suicides have I responded to throughout my career? Each was a jarring reminder of life's fragility and the depths of human despair. The graphic scenes, the anguished cries of loved ones left behind - these images linger in the recesses of my mind, a silent testament to the toll that this profession exacts upon the mortal soul.

And what of the accidents and fatalities have I witnessed? How many times have I stood at the scene of a devastating crash, grappling with the harsh reality of lives cut short in an instant? The faces of children and infants, innocent victims of circumstance, are forever etched into the fabric of my consciousness. The domestic violence incidents, the brutal homicides - each one a stark reminder of the darkness that lurks just beneath the surface of society.

There is more than tragedy and loss; another layer of pain often goes unseen - the personal struggles we carry to our calls. I have known fellow officers who have dealt with untimely deaths within their own families while simultaneously grappling with the burden of their professional responsibility. They are parents, they are spouses, and they are children who were also dealing with loss. How does one pause thinking about trauma in their own life, even for a moment so that they can deal with another while on call?

Yet, despite this profession's toll on us, resilience runs deep within the fabric of law enforcement. I have watched my fellow officers, who were once brimming with vigor and idealism, navigate the treacherous waters of this profession, only to emerge battered and bruised on the other side. Physically and emotionally exhausted, they continue to soldier on, their resolve unbroken by the storms surrounding them.

Some officers across the nation have faced cancer and other threatening diseases, confronting mortality head-on as they continue to serve under the most challenging of conditions. It is a testament to the indomitable spirit in the hearts of those who wear the badge, a spirit that refuses to be extinguished by the darkness surrounding us.

As I near the twilight of my career in law enforcement, I am confronted by the physical toll that twenty-five-plus years of service have exacted upon my body. Some of my colleagues have undergone hip and knee replacements and then been forced to return to the job with lingering limitations. (Or, in some cases, not allowed to return at all.) The simple act of getting in and out of a patrol car while being weighed down by our heavy gun belts becomes a daily struggle and a physical reminder of the sacrifices we make in service to our communities.

Beyond the physical toll on our bodies, we carry a mental and emotional burden each day. I've seen many colleagues escorted to their career exit because they violated policy or succumbed to the relentless stress of the job.

In the lexicon of law enforcement, the term "cop-out" takes on a deeper meaning - an evasion, an escape from facing up to the reality of leaving this profession. Many of us stay too long, tethered to this job by financial obligations, our identities irrevocably tied to the badge, or simply out of fear of what lies beyond the confines of this calling.

As I reflect on my journey, I am reminded of the importance of cultivating an identity that extends beyond the confines of law enforcement. Before I donned the uniform, I was a Certified Nursing Assistant and a Mental Health Tech and held various roles in the service industry. In these roles, I discovered my passion for helping others, which only deepened when I received the calling to serve in law enforcement.

The uniform gave me a newfound sense of purpose, allowing me to serve my fellow citizens in a different capacity. But as I navigate the final chapters of my career, I am acutely aware of the importance of having an identity that transcends the badge - an identity rooted in compassion, empathy, and a deep-seated desire to make a difference in the lives of others.

I stand committed to helping my fellow officers identify their trauma and navigate the complexities of this profession with resilience and grace. This profession requires us to confront the darkness within ourselves and acknowledge the toll on our bodies, minds, spirits, and families. But it also holds the promise of healing, growth, and a renewed sense of purpose beyond the confines of law enforcement.

Question: What keeps you on the job? Will you be ready to leave when it is time?

Throughout my 26 years in law enforcement, I've found solace and wisdom in Simon Sinek's writings, particularly his works like "Start with Why" and "Leaders Eat Last." Sinek's teachings center around understanding our "Why"—the purpose behind our actions and the driving force that fuels our commitment to service.

As law enforcement officers, we are all leaders in our own right. From the moment we raise our right hands and swear to uphold the Constitution, we accept the mantle of leadership, becoming servants and protectors of our communities. It's incumbent upon us to lead with our "Why" so we may understand the motivations behind our actions and those of the people we encounter.

Why do people act the way they do toward law enforcement? It's a question without a simple answer. Understanding the "Why" behind a person's behavior often provides insight into who they are and lays the groundwork for meaningful conversations—as peacekeepers, understanding a person "Why" can help us approach situations with empathy and compassion rather than reacting with anger or frustration.

I've learned that losing sight of our "Why" can lead us astray. When I ask our deputies in training why they get up and come to work each day, some respond with, "Because I have bills to pay." While this may be true, the paycheck is merely a byproduct of our work (Simon Sinek), and we must never forget that our true purpose lies in serving and protecting our communities. How long do you think an officer would last if the only "Why" were getting paid twice a month?

In the depths of my career, I've grappled with the profound question of my "Why." This driving force compels me to rise each morning, even on the darkest days when the world's weight seems too heavy to bear. My "Why" has always been rooted in service to others, a guiding principle that has shaped every facet of my professional journey.

From the humble beginnings of my career, working the drive-thru at Wendy's Hamburger or serving as a Certified Nursing Assistant at a nursing home, I've always placed the needs of others above my own. Since day one, this philosophy has been ingrained in me as a fundamental belief that has defined my approach to life and work.

Yet, despite my unwavering commitment to service, there have been moments when I've faltered when the darkness threatened to engulf me, and my "Why" seemed insufficient to light the way. In those moments of doubt and despair, I've had to reach deep within myself, to the day when I first raised my right hand and swore to uphold the Constitution of the United States of America and the State of Florida.

There have been days when my "Why" has been tested, when the very people I swore to serve have questioned my motives, failed to appreciate my efforts, and even attempted to walk over me when given a chance. But in those moments of adversity, my "Why" has also been my most significant source of strength, a beacon of light that has guided me through those moments.

It's a reminder that our "Why" is not just a fleeting emotion or a passing fancy - it's a deeply ingrained belief that transcends the trials and tribulations of our profession. It's a reminder that even in the face of adversity, even when the darkness threatens to consume us, our "Why" remains our North Star, guiding us on the path to honor, integrity, and service to others.

As I look back on my career, I am reminded of the importance of reconnecting with our "Why"—the driving force that compels us to rise each morning and face the challenges of the day with courage and conviction. Understanding our "Why" gives us the strength to navigate the complexities of our profession, confront our trauma, and emerge more robust, resilient, and compassionate than ever before.

Question: What is your 'Why'? How often do you remind yourself of your 'Why?' Do you remember to remind yourself?

Chapter Four

My Story: I'm Sticking to It

Growing up in the small town of Bunnell on the east coast of Florida, the 1970s were a magical time for me—a time I remember as the "best decade for a kid to grow up." It was a simple time before the crack epidemic cast its dark shadow over our community. In those days, life was what I affectionately called 'country living.'

My childhood was filled with simple pleasures; I was surrounded by 'tree candy' - orange, tangerine, and blackberry trees in my grandparent's yard. There were also numerous animals - ducks, chickens, and a pen housing a couple of giant hogs. These were the days when elder folks would reminisce about the 'good ole' days.'

I vividly remember chasing chickens out of my grandparents' cabbage and collard greens garden, playing hide-and-seek in the woods surrounding their home, and collecting soda bottles from around town to trade in for candy and NEHI soda. My preteen years, especially the period of fifth grade in 1978, stand out as some of my most cherished memories.

We didn't have many material possessions, but we made up for what we lacked in wealth with the ability to entertain ourselves. We'd spend hours playing basketball on the outside courts provided to us by the government. One 'lucky kid' always shared his football to toss around. Unlike today, we kids were free to roam the fields in the projects, meet friends to choose teams, and play without fearing the police being called.

These memories of my childhood serve as a stark contrast to the challenges I would face later in life, particularly as the crack epidemic ravaged our community and altered the trajectory of my life. The lessons and experiences of my formative years have shaped me into the person I am today - a person committed to helping others navigate their trauma and find healing and resilience in the face of adversity.

Reflecting on those days of carefree childhood, I can't help but cringe at the recklessness - or perhaps, the bravery - with which we played football in the fields of the projects. The open field should have been cleared of any broken soda bottles or discarded metal that could cause harm, but instead, we dove into the game with reckless abandon. Many of us left the field with bleeding feet from running barefoot or being tackled on broken RC Cola bottles that abruptly ended our game. Even with a team member down, we would regroup and pick up the game in a day or two, undeterred by the possible injuries to ourselves.

I wasn't the fastest kid at ten, but I loved running. In the middle of summer, my best friends and I would race in the streets, kicking off our shoes in the hopes of running faster - only to feel the searing pain of the blacktop burning our feet. Perhaps the pain fueled our determination to reach the finish line, where a friend stood with arms outstretched. The rule was simple: the winner was the first to touch the designated person's hand. After reaching the finish line, we'd sprint off the road into the grass to cool off our blistered feet as quickly as possible.

Growing up in a family of ten, we lived in a small three-bedroom, one-bath home. The five boys shared one room, the three girls shared another, and my parents had their own. We didn't have hot water, so my mom would heat water on the stove for my younger brother and me to take a bath, a routine normal in many homes in our neighborhood.

Both of my parents worked hard to make ends meet. My father was a skilled mechanic, and my mother dedicated herself to nursing as a Licensed Practical Nurse (LPN). Despite dual incomes, luxuries were few and far between for our large family. We didn't have the latest toys showcased in the Sears catalog. I have clear memories of times when my youngest brother, Ross, and I would sit together, flipping through the pages and playfully claiming ownership of the items we saw. We never harbored envy or jealousy for what we couldn't have. Those toys, we thought, were for "white people." We were matter-of-factly accepting of our circumstances and found contentment in the simple joys of childhood.

One of my fondest memories from those days was our knack for putting together bikes from abandoned ones we found on the side of the road. We'd venture into the 'white side' of town across Moody Boulevard, scavenging for discarded bicycles and other treasures left out for garbage pickup. With ingenuity and teamwork, we learned how to transform several broken bikes into a single functioning one.

As my friends and I entered middle school, our interests shifted to organized sports like basketball and football. I found myself drawn to running. By seventh grade, sprinting in elementary school evolved into a passion for distance running by seventh grade. A couple of friends and I even went as far as purposely missing the school bus so we could jog the three miles back home to our neighborhood, much to the bewilderment of our neighbors.

As a seventh-grader, the concept of a "Runner's High" was foreign to me. Yet, looking back, I remember the serene calmness that enveloped me during long runs to nowhere in particular. Little did I know then that running would become a cornerstone of my life's journey, both as a person searching for identity and as a law enforcement officer grappling with trauma.

Growing up in a close-knit community where elementary and junior/senior high schools shared a campus, I found another community by joining the track team. While running in circles didn't initially resonate with me, I looked forward to the camaraderie it offered. Despite competing against older juniors and seniors during track and field season, I viewed it as an opportunity to challenge myself and strive for personal improvement.

For me, running wasn't just about competition; it was an escape. It provided precious moments of solitude, a respite from the chaos of life. Sometimes, I ran without a goal or destination in mind. I didn't rely on fancy gadgets to track my progress; I ran purely for the sake of running.

I found clarity and peace in those moments, with the pounding of the pavement beneath my feet. Running became my sanctuary, a place where I could dream and find peace in the rhythm of my breath. Little did I know then that these early experiences with running would become a metaphor for my journey through life and law enforcement. They taught me the importance of perseverance, self-discipline, and finding moments of stillness. As I continued to navigate the complexities of trauma and resilience, running would remain a steadfast companion, guiding me through the darkest of days and reminding me of the strength that lies within.

The End of Innocence

As the 1970s drew to a close, so did my childhood, fading into the horizon like a distant memory. The dawn of the 1980s felt like my world was headed into an impending storm that offered no refuge or respite from what was to come. It was a storm unlike any we had weathered before, sweeping our community and nation with an unforgiving intensity.

The early 1980s marked the arrival of crack cocaine in our small town, casting a shadow over our once-idyllic surroundings. Even as a young observer, I witnessed the gradual transformation of our peaceful 'country living' into a landscape marred by despair and decay. Lives were unraveling, families were torn apart, and violence became an all-too-familiar presence.

The impact of crack cocaine was like nothing anyone had ever seen, casting darkness over our streets even in the daylight. People I once knew became hollow shells of their former selves; their eyes haunted by desperation for the poison they craved. It was during this tumultuous time that I experienced my first encounter with death, and it hit inside my own home with the loss of my fifteen-year-old brother Marvin to suicide. This devastating blow left our family reeling with grief and anguish. I was 13. Right before he committed suicide, he gave me a letter to give to my mother. He asked not to open it, and minutes later, he died at his own hands. I carried that burden for years.

I was no stranger to the sound of gunshots echoing through the woods, a familiar backdrop to my childhood spent hunting with my father. On one particular evening, a sudden burst of gunfire shattered the quiet night, jolting me from my sleep with a mixture of fear and curiosity as I ran to investigate.

I sprinted toward the crowd in front of a nearby duplex, my heart pounding as I made my way through the crowd of onlookers. Peering through the people, I caught sight of a man lying on the ground, his shirt completely soaked with blood. It was another grim reminder of the harsh realities that lurked just beyond the safety of my front door.

The images of my brother and that dead man would haunt me in the days and weeks that followed. I barely knew that family, but I felt as if I understood their pain, as my own family had experienced our recent loss. These incidents served as a vivid reminder of how violence had now replaced our once-idyllic community.

In the aftermath of those traumatic events, my parents made the difficult decision to uproot our family in search of a fresh start. We packed our belongings and embarked on a journey to Gainesville, Florida, leaving behind the familiar for what we hoped to be a brighter future. Once again, I turned to running to find peace. I found solace in the simple act, a form of therapy that allowed me to (once again) escape the pain and grief that weighed heavily on my young shoulders. I settled into my new surroundings, loving my new, middle-class neighborhood. I effortlessly forged connections with my peers and enjoyed the peaceful rhythm of daily life.

In the quiet moments spent running, I could overcome any obstacles in my path. As I navigated my teen years, putting one foot before the other became more than just a hobby; it became my lifeline, a reliable companion in times of joy and sorrow. I carried the lessons learned on those solitary runs, drawing upon the resilience and determination that had brought me through the darkest moments of my youth.

I transitioned into my teenage years, a new chapter filled with excitement and uncertainty. My eighth-grade year at Howard Bishop Middle School passed in a blur (as moments in childhood often do). Before I knew it, a new era began at Buchholz High School. This was a school beckoning with the promise of opportunities, chief among them my foray into competitive running. Joining the cross country and track team, I immersed myself in these sports, and each training session was a testament to the dedication and discipline required to excel in the sport and acted as a distraction from my past.

As a freshman navigating the complexities of high school life, I became obsessed with nutrition, stretches, and warm-ups, eager to reach my peak performance. With each passing day, my endurance grew, my strides lengthened, and I found myself traversing distances that once seemed impossible, a tangible reward for my efforts.

Throughout my high school career, I embraced my role as a competitive yet unassuming runner, consistently contributing points to our team without becoming a liability. I may not have been among our school's most elite athletes, but I took pride in my ability to hold my own on the track and cross-country events, earning the respect of my teammates and coaches alike.

Beyond athletics, I found companionship in unexpected places, immersing myself in the various social scenes of high school and connecting with peers from all walks of life. Despite the occasional skirmish and scuffle, I navigated the waters of adolescence with relative ease, my quick wit and infectious humor serving as a shield against bullying and ridicule.

If I were to describe my alignment with a group in high school, it would likely be the theater nerds. Those were my people, the kooky dreamers who shared a pursuit of knowledge and creativity. We enjoyed engaging in extracurricular activities like acting, improvisation, and drama club, I honed my comedic timing and storytelling prowess, developed the ability to captivate an audience, and loved every aspect of the stage.

High school was my period of growth and self-discovery, marked by many triumphs. Reflecting on those formative years, I am grateful for the resilience that carried me through the trials of earlier adolescence, paving the way for my future. As the curtain closed on my high school years, I found myself standing at the doorstep of adulthood, uncertain of the path ahead.

Unlike my father, whose technical prowess shaped his career as an auto mechanic, I lacked the aptitude for that line of work. With no clear direction, I embarked on a series of transient jobs in the fast-food industry, each offering meager wages and fleeting satisfaction.

My journey into the world of fast food began at a Chinese restaurant, where I worked behind the counter, grappling with orders and navigating the frantic pace of a busy kitchen. From there, I drifted from one fast-food chain to another, chasing after incremental pay raises that offered little in the way of true purpose. I longed for something more, a way forward, transcending the monotony of flipping burgers and taking orders.

As I wrestled with the difficult transition to adulthood, I found myself capturing a specific memory of my mother's career as a Registered Nurse. I recalled the ritual that was my contribution to our busy family – carefully ironing my mom's pristine white uniforms. I witnessed her pride when she walked out the door each morning and headed to a job she loved and others respected. This led me to wonder if I should also pursue a healthcare career.

Luckily, fate had other plans for me. Despite my earnest aspirations, the path to a career in nursing was difficult. I didn't have the discipline to sit through the required college classes and became bored with medical lectures. I found myself adrift once again. However, I remained steadfast in my resolve to carve out a future defined by purpose and passion.

Question: Was there a single or multiple event that impacted your life for the better or worse?

Chapter Five

The Road to Law Enforcement

In the late 1980s, a friend introduced me to the field of Certified Nursing Assistant (CNA). At the time, the healthcare industry needed compassionate caregivers, and the entry requirements were minimal—a state exam without the need for formal classes. Despite lacking a specialized skill set, earning $7.50 to $8.50 per hour in a field dedicated to caring for others was both enticing and promising.

Becoming a CNA proved to be one of the most fulfilling experiences of my life. Working with the elderly nearing the end of their lives, I provided comfort and companionship during their final days. Many under my care shared their life stories—tales of triumphs and regrets, moments of joy and sorrow. Families expressed gratitude for treating their loved ones with the utmost respect and dignity, acknowledging the bond between caregiver and patient.

As a CNA, I rediscovered the profound power of compassion and empathy. While these already existed within me, the daily practice of tending to the needs of others allowed humility and gratitude to permeate my thoughts. I took immense pride in my work, approaching each day with purpose and dedication to those in my care.

Both my parents had instilled in me a strong work ethic, a trait passed down from their parents. I wholeheartedly embraced the demands of my new role as a CNA, often working double shifts multiple times a week without hesitation. My extensive and physically capable stature, along with a profound sense of caring (and quick humor), eventually led to another role - Mental Health Tech.

As a Mental Health Tech, I worked alongside counselors in group settings, supporting and assisting individuals struggling with mental health challenges. In moments of crisis, I helped maintain order and, when necessary, intervened physically to ensure the safety of both clients and staff. This role demanded patience, resilience, and a deep sense of empathy—a natural extension of the caregiving principles I had embraced as a CNA.

Through these experiences, I learned the importance of empathy and Emotional Intelligence in providing adequate care to those in need. Each encounter, whether with a terminally ill patient or a troubled individual seeking mental health services, reinforced the value of human connection and the transformative power of compassion.

As Mental Health Tech, I was thrust into the tumultuous world of individuals who were grappling with some of the most severe mental health issues. I began my work in a mental health hospital unit where they housed juveniles who had committed sexual violence. The stories of these young souls, both victims and perpetrators, weighed heavily on my heart, their experiences serving as a constant reminder of how deep-rooted pain can consume human lives and leave destruction.

In my early twenties as a Mental Health Tech, I honed valuable de-escalation skills, recognizing the importance of defusing volatile situations with empathy and sensitivity. My de-escalation training and physical restraint techniques helped create a safe and supportive environment for those in crisis.

At the age of twenty-four, I entered a new chapter of my life with the union of my second marriage and the arrival of a beautiful daughter shortly afterward. Yet, despite the joy of parenthood, financial strains began to take their toll. My then-wife and I found ourselves navigating the challenges of unemployment, forced to move in with her mother as we struggled with our future.

The confines of a stagnant wage and limited opportunities weighed heavily on my shoulders. As the sole provider for my new family, I knew I needed to chart a course that would afford us the stability and security we longed for. This realization dawned upon me during quiet contemplation on a Sunday morning in January of 1997—a pivotal moment of clarity propelling me toward a new career.

Sitting in the mental health hospital hallway with my colleague Mike, we conversed about our stagnant careers that were taking a toll on us. We both understood that our current trajectory was unsustainable. Looking through classified ads in the Sunday paper, our eyes scanned for any hope of a better life. Then, Mike stumbled upon an ad from the state of Florida—an opportunity that promised a path to stability and security as Correctional Officer Trainees.

The prospect of a five-month paid training program to become correctional officers, accompanied by a substantial increase in salary and enhanced benefits, ignited a spark of hope. It was an opportunity to chart a course toward a fulfilling career that would provide for my family.

The initial excitement of this newfound prospect soon waned for Mike, and his resolve began to falter. A man of words rather than action, he retreated into the safety of familiarity, unwilling to venture beyond the comfort zone of his current employment. Despite our shared enthusiasm at the outset, our paths diverged as I remained steadfast in my determination to seize this chance for a better life.

On the morning of my interview, I was a mixture of anticipation and nerves. I made sure my only suit was immaculate. After drinking my second cup of coffee, I headed to my interview on the hour-and-a-half journey. Arriving at the parking area, the state prison complex appeared larger than life. I was met with a scene of eager applicants, each vying for limited positions at the prison. There must have been fifty or more applicants headed into the prison along with me.

I entered the prison with feelings of immediate self-doubt, looking at the other candidates and regretting my choice. I tried my best to channel the positive voices I knew resided inside of me: my father and mother, my coaches. I allowed those voices to be the gifts to propel me forward. As I approached the registration desk, I was determined to embrace the opportunity before me.

Seated before the interview board, a trio of faces sat before me—faces of authority and scrutiny. Yet, a sense of calm began to guide my responses with a clarity born of conviction.

Among the barrage of questions, a singular one stood out—a simple yet profound one that bore the weight of expectation: "How would you respond to an order given to you by a female supervisor?" In that moment, I drew upon the lessons gleaned from years of service in healthcare, where gender held no dominion over competence or authority. Without hesitation, I articulated a belief forged in my experience—a testament to leadership, unbound by gender constraints. As my words found their mark, I watched as smiles crossed the faces of the board members, their pens dancing across their evaluation forms.

For me, this was not merely an exercise in rhetoric but a reflection of a sincerely held conviction rooted in my upbringing and nurtured by the wisdom of formidable female leaders like my mother, my grandmother, and other strong women who had illuminated my path.

Days turned into weeks as I waited for an answer, and a sense of uncertainty crept into my subconscious. The deafening silence from the state prison left me with the lingering questions, "Are my dreams dashed?" and "What's next?"

This was not merely a fleeting setback; it was a crossroads, a juncture where the trajectory of my future hung in the balance. My dream of becoming a correctional officer was not just a fly-by-night decision. No, it had emerged as a beacon of hope amidst the uncertainty of my current situation.

I spent this time in wait, reflecting on the journey that had led me to this moment. I moved toward the Firefighter's Academy shortly after high school eight years prior. The fire academy had been but a fleeting chapter in my journey, punctuated by unfulfilled aspirations and dashed dreams. Having graduated from the academy and passed their state exam, I applied to agencies across Florida, only to be placed on a long waiting list with other hopefuls. I finally grasped the reality of my circumstances and the lofty ideals that had once animated my ambitions. It was not to be.

But now, as my financial obligations loomed, the prospect of hearing back from the state prison assumed unparalleled significance. It was not merely a job offer but a lifeline that promised to propel me from the suffocating embrace of stagnation and possible poverty toward a brighter future.

The notion of confining individuals behind bars was the farthest from my aspirations. Yet, fate had woven a tapestry of twists and turns, leading me to the doors of a state prison. The prospect of being a corrections officer seemed inconceivable as the stakes were high, not merely in terms of financial rewards but also in self-validation and personal fulfillment. Deep inside, I yearned to transcend the limitations of my circumstances and forge a path toward self-actualization.

As I awaited the fateful message from the state prison, I couldn't shake the sense of urgency that overwhelmed me. I realized my desire for professional advancement was a quest for redemption—a chance to honor the memory of my departed father and carve out a legacy worthy of his enduring pride.

Then came the phone call summoning me to the human resource office of Lake Correctional Institute. The journey that once seemed unattainable now opened up a world of possibilities.

As I stepped into the state prison for my first shift as an uncertified trainee, fear mingled with curiosity gripped my senses. Surrounded by a crew of fellow trainees, each harboring their hopes and apprehensions, I awaited the tour of the prison grounds that promised to unveil the enigmatic world within.

I was led by a grizzly sergeant whose expressions bore the weight of countless war stories etched in the annals of time, and the tour was one that I would remember—the sights, the smells, and the emotions of the inmates. Each corridor and cell bore witness to the complexities of the human condition—a microcosm of society's underbelly concealed behind imposing walls of steel and stone.

Yet, amongst the specter of incarceration and the echoes of past transgressions, a profound sense of duty stirred within me. Before attending the academy, I felt a sense of pride in wearing the uniform. I had become part of a brotherhood that stood against the encroaching tide of lawlessness and chaos that threatened to engulf the fabric of society.

In the sweltering heat of June, I commenced a new chapter of my journey—a baptism by fire of sorts: the Corrections Academy. Once again tasked with navigating the classroom and embracing the legal intricacies and procedural protocols, I found a passion for the rigors of training and a genuine determination to succeed. As days bled into weeks, the relentless cadence of training forged bonds of camaraderie with my classmates from all walks of life.

The Academy

The drumbeat of discipline echoed through the corridors within the academy. It was a symphony of rigidity that mirrored the paramilitary of institute law enforcement. Each day unfurled with the precision of a well-oiled machine, punctuated by the cadence of uniform inspections, the code of ethics, and the solemn reminder of those who paved the path before us.

As recruits, we became disciplined in the code of conduct. It was our Bible, one that demanded unwavering deference to authority. A mere glance from a seasoned corrections officer or law enforcement veteran elicited a reflexive response—an acknowledgment of their rank and experience rendered through a ceremonial exchange of honor. Yet, beneath protocol and etiquette, lived a palpable undercurrent of apprehension. Their years of expertise came with the scars of countless battles, and our instructors made sure to impart lessons steeped in cautionary tales of the perils that awaited us at the prison.

The warnings were stern reminders of the types of people we would soon be guarding. They warned us that there was a distinct line between inmate and officer, a line that could become blurred over time. The fear our instructors and supervisors instilled within us was not born out of malice but rather a solemn duty to prepare us for the grim realities that awaited beyond the confines of the training academy.

The melting pot of diverse backgrounds and experiences of my coworkers forged bonds that transcended the superficial barriers of race and gender. Yet, beneath the camaraderie lay a shared understanding of the weighty responsibility that rested upon our shoulders—the custodianship of those whose behavior stood as a testament to the darker recesses of humanity.

Each day, as we navigated the rigors of training, there were constant tales and an ever-present reminder of the fragility of life within the unforgiving landscape of the prison system. Yet, we found solace in the collective strength of our resolve—a steadfast commitment to uphold the values of the justice system and integrity that formed the bedrock of our profession.

Fear and determination fueled me as I progressed in my training. The thought of failure always loomed in the back of my mind, casting its ominous shadow over my every task. I was haunted by the fear of reverting to the confines of my past, the soul-crushing jobs—a fate I was determined to evade at all costs.

Though I had my trials and tribulations, both professionally and personally, I also bore witness to the loss of those ill-equipped to withstand the rigors of the academy. Some faltered under the weight of family obligations, their dreams eclipsed by the harsh reality of life's demands. Others succumbed to the allure of complacency, their aspirations falling prey to mediocrity.

Through five long months of training, most of my class conquered every task. —driven by an unyielding resolve to carve our destiny instead of leaving it in the hands of fate. They understood that mere attendance was not enough, that success demanded a genuine dedication to excellence that transcended the confines of the academy walls.

Prison to Jail

Stepping onto the prison grounds during the night shift, I was thrust into a world where darkness was not just literal. The night shift seemed to bring out the worst misconduct in inmates: gambling, physical violence, sexual violence. On my first night, one of my duties was to perform rounds and call in my head count. I was assigned to a training officer, and we were both responsible for the care, custody, and control of over one hundred inmates. It was early morning when an inmate exited one of the shower stalls, covered in blood and appearing to be the victim of an attack by another inmate. However, we discovered that he had cut both of his wrists. He was silent as he attempted to pull the veins of his wrists.

My training officer grabbed the first aid kit, and we brought him to the floor to render immediate aid.

Fear gnawed at the edges of my consciousness. Not the fear of the inmates but the fear of my inadequacy. The academy had armed me with knowledge but a paltry defense against the onslaught of shenanigans that awaited me nightly as I entered the prison walls. I quickly realized that the academy had been a mere prologue—a prelude of things to come.

While working my shifts at the prison, I was exposed to certain 'cat and mouse games.' The inmates, seasoned veterans of manipulation, sought to prey upon the vulnerabilities of the new trainees. They were adept at spotting weakness and exploiting it for their amusement. Through all their manipulation attempts, I clung to the resilience I honed through years of pain and loss during my formative years. During my experience in mental health centers, I had already navigated those treacherous waters with a steely resolve not to become easily distracted by deceit.

As days turned into weeks and weeks became months, another old talent of mine proved helpful. This one served me in the darkest of nights. My gift of listening became a lifeline amidst the tumult of the midnight shift—a sanctuary for those who sought to lay down their burden. In the stillness of the night, I became a confidant and silent witness to the stories of the inmates.

In the unforgiving embrace of the state prison, I found myself a transient rookie navigating a world that was more demanding and less forgiving than I had ever imagined. My new law enforcement family felt more like an exclusive club where rookies were tolerated at best, and conformity overshadowed camaraderie. To make matters worse, the 90-minute drive home after every grueling shift became a dangerous ritual. The road became a rhythmic lullaby of tires on asphalt, my struggle against drowsiness in the early mornings. The realization struck that this pace was unsustainable. I longed for a sense of belonging and an end to the fatigue of treacherous driving. These circumstances led me to seek an alternative: the next chapter in my law enforcement journey.

A fellow trainee, whom I considered a comrade in the trenches of the state prison, extended an invitation to apply at the county jail. He described a Utopian picture of correctional officers, boasting a twelve-hour shift with two days on and two days off, a schedule that promised respite and a semblance of normalcy. He boasted unlimited overtime and assurances of a safer and more professional environment. It was time to move to greener pastors.

In December 1997, I entered the county jail, a newfound haven for my law enforcement aspirations. My comrade hadn't lied. The new schedule was a release for my tired soul. Two days on, two days off, and the rhythm of my new life began. I felt as though I had found my tribe. The professional ambiance of the county jail was a welcome departure from the harsh realities of the state prison.

Armed with a radio and the weight of responsibility, I embraced my role as a corrections officer in the county jail. The housing units echoed with the onslaught and shuffle of up to ninety inmates. I felt appropriately armed with my communication skills, and my time at the state prison was an asset. I did not carry a weapon, just a radio and the power of effective communication.

Even in my new surroundings, my mental health tech training continued to be useful. The art of active listening became my 'super suit,' a skill honed through a lifetime of observation. This skill proved indispensable in the daily dance of officer-inmate interactions.

The county jail became more than just a workplace. In the echoes of the housing unit, I discovered the power of words and the strength that comes from understanding. The narrative of my law enforcement journey was evolving. I found a community, a family forged in our daily struggles, dreams, and victories. The bonds formed within those walls endure to this day, a testament to the enduring camaraderie of law enforcement.

In the confines of the county jail, the mantra of care, custody, and control became a principle that helped guide me. Unlike the state prison, where the guilty would serve years, if not the remainder of their lives, the county jail housed a population where innocence prevailed for the majority until otherwise determined. Most of these individuals were still awaiting their day in court, their fate still hanging in the balance.

Yet, like the state prison, the currents of manipulation persisted, although on a much smaller scale. In the booking unit, I encountered individuals in crisis during the intake and processing—the broken, the lost, the addicted, and the dispossessed. Whether it was the DUI detainee or a first-time domestic violence offender, each bore the weight of their circumstances, their frustrations often leading to confrontation with those in uniform.

For many, the jail became a revolving door. Repeat offenders were celebrated by their fellow inmates, and their return to incarceration was hailed as a badge of honor. To some, the jail became a rite of passage and familiar waypoint in the tumultuous journey of their lives.

Among the thousands of detainees over the years, I witnessed the plight of our youth. It was a sobering reminder of the harsh realities that transcended age. Juveniles as young as fourteen were thrust into the penal system, their innocence lost amidst the harsh realities of a world that showed no mercy. I can still recall the sadness looking into their eyes; I could see their inevitable future. I've looked into the eyes of some of these same young men a decade later as they re-entered the jail on their way to prison.

In the juvenile pod of the county jail, I was confronted with the reality of youthful transgression and its consequences. Teenagers, barely removed from childhood innocence, who faced the grim realities of life. Adjudicated as adults and awaiting trial, many of these young souls were on the precipice of a life defined by decades of imprisonment. Yet, amidst their confinement, they laughed and played card games, seemingly oblivious to the gravity of their circumstances. Charged with violent crimes ranging from home invasions to murder, they inhabited a world where the weight of their actions seemed lost on them, their laughter a defiant echo in the face of their impending fate.

In the county jail, my sense of humor emerged as both shield and weapon—a tool honed through years of dealing with those in crisis. With quick wit and improvisational skills, I defused tense situations. I navigated the delicate balance of maintaining order while fostering a sense of humanity within the confines of the jail walls. Firm but fair, I employed humor as a means of correction and connection, recognizing the need to connect with inmates on a human level, even amidst the harsh realities of incarceration.

Outside the jail walls, when the sound of inmates had ceased, trauma awaited me in the form of unseen demons lurking in the shadows of the parking lot. Behind the facade of laughter and humor, I grappled with the weight of my personal experiences and the emotional toll of bearing witness to the brokenness of humanity, including my own.

Throughout my tenure at the county jail, I became known as the 'good' officer, or the 'funny' officer. I was the guy who appeared to be in a good mood for the inmates and my co-workers. Yet, beneath my humor and positive attitude lay the unspoken truth of the toll that all my trauma exacted—a truth hidden behind my laughter, was my trauma waiting to be acknowledged and addressed. In the shadow of my struggles, I found purpose in helping others navigate their trauma, forging connections, and fostering understanding through navigating the human experience together.

Question: What Challenges did you face when you first entered the profession? Did you observe any challenges if you are a spouse or other family member?

Chapter Six

Demons: All Hell Broke Loose

Working twelve-hour shifts at the county jail gave me moments to reflect on my life. However, instead of living in gratitude, the voices in my head kicked up my demons. I navigated my career in law enforcement while the suffocating weight of sadness engulfed me, fueled by a sense of inadequacy and disappointment that constantly occupied my thinking.

Though my professional life appeared to be moving forward, the echoes of my failures in my personal life reverberated with loud clarity. By 1998, I found myself separated from my second wife, our union fractured by the strains of distance, personal conflicts and the relentless demands of my career. Living in one county while traversing the next to pick up my daughter, every moment spent apart from her was a dagger to my heart, a reminder of the chasm that separated me from the idyllic image of fatherhood I had once envisioned.

My young daughter bore witness to the fractured fragments of my life, which included not always being present. She sometimes asked me, "Dad, why are you sad?" I continued to suffer with a sense of grief. Throughout my interactions with my daughter, I always wore a mask. As the years passed by so fast, one of my greatest regrets was not always being present. My father's legacy loomed large, casting a long shadow over my journey. Comparisons to his steadfast devotion and unwavering commitment to family reminded me of the standards I feared I could never meet.

If you change nothing, then nothing changes. I recalled trying to convince myself that things would get better. I didn't know it then; However, I do not doubt that I would have been diagnosed with depression. It was a depression that I carried with me daily, disguised as happiness. By 1999, the weight became almost unbearable; I found myself struggling to get out of bed. It became a struggle to put on the uniform. There were times when I would get dressed for work yet called in sick because the pain was unbearable.

On the rare occasions when I found an escape from the demands of my career and the tragedies of my personal life, I sought escape in the loud and smokey confines of a karaoke bar, where the loud music and haze of alcohol allowed me to detach from myself and the onslaught of my demons. I was a different person among the laughter and clinking of glasses. I found what I thought was peace from the suffocating grip of my thoughts, drowning my sorrows in a sea of bourbon and beer.

Through the haze of intoxication, the demons lurked around the edges of my mind, a constant reminder that the failures in my personal life were real, and neither Jim Beam nor Jack Daniels could save me. Closing time was the worst part of the night. The crowds would thin, and I would have to reconnect with my reality. It was then when I found myself being escorted to my car by my demons. I constantly wondered why I couldn't out run them.

Running away from my Demons

As the years passed since my father's death, the weight of my struggles grew heavier, burdening me with a sense of isolation and despair that seemed impossible to carry. In a bid to escape the suffocating grip of my mind, I made the difficult decision to uproot my life and seek a new start with my family up north. My mother and youngest brother were residing in Delaware and I saw an opportunity for a fresh start, a chance to leave behind the ghosts of my past and begin anew.

With a heavy heart, I said my goodbyes to my family at the jail. Their well-wishes would remain with me my entire journey up north. The Major's parting words gave me a sense of hope. He thanked me for my hard work and dedication to the profession. He further reminded me that I would always have a home if I chose to return. It was a bittersweet reminder of the home I was leaving behind and the uncertain future ahead.

Transitioning was one of the most challenging decisions I had to make from both a personal and a professional point of view. One of the most memorable moments came when I stood on the train station platform, my ex-wife, and our young daughter by my side. As I embraced her, I found peace and pain simultaneously; her innocent smile determined me to build a life for her and always be a part of her life. With tears streaming down my face, I held her close, savoring every precious moment before reluctantly boarding the train that would carry me away from her embrace.

As the train rattled along the tracks, the rhythmic motion of the journey distracted me from where I was leaving and where I was headed. Lost in the pages of a book, I sought shelter from my thoughts. My heart had begun to ache, and the memory of my daughter's smile was a constant presence in my mind.

Finally, as the train pulled into the station in Newark, Delaware, I was greeted by the familiar faces of my mother and youngest brother; their presence was what my exhausted body and spirit needed. Hugging my mom, I found a glimmer of hope that maybe I had made the right choice. Their presence reminded me of how vital family is in our darkest moments. Perhaps this will be the new beginning that I needed.

In one of the coldest winters in thirty years in Delaware, I grappled with the bitter chill of loneliness and uncertainty. With no cell phones to bridge the distance between us, I needed to hear from my ex-wife, needing to hear that our daughter was ok, maybe looking for reassurance that I had made the right choice. When I finally spoke to her, she shared the story of our daughter's tearful protest at the train station. Our daughter wanted her mother to wait for the train to come back. The story shattered my heart, not only reminding me of my failure but also a stark reminder of the profound impact of my absence on the one I held most dear.

As I navigated the unfamiliar terrain of my new surroundings, the biting cold of the winter air served as a cruel testament to the harsh realities of my decision. Accustomed to the balmy embrace of Florida's climate, I was ill-prepared for Delaware's unforgiving cold. A chance encounter at a grocery store, where a casual remark about the frigid temperatures sent shivers down my spine, served as a sobering reminder of the stark contrast between the familiarity of my past and the alien landscape of my present.

Struggling to find my footing on the frost-covered pavement, I couldn't help but feel like a fish out of water as I embraced my new reality. I felt like a mere shadow of my former self as I constantly cursed the cold and continued to second-guess my decision to leave Florida. Once again, I could hear the chilling laughter of my imagined demons; I heard them mock me with my insecurities, mocking my feeble attempts to navigate the treacherous terrain of my new reality.

Days after my arrival were filled with negative self-talk. "What were you thinking, leaving a secure job?" and "You are never going to make it up here; you are a nobody." At 31 years of age, I still felt lost. My mornings would consist of coffee and classified ads. During this time, I realized that I had made a decision based on emotions, thinking I could escape who I was by running away. At this moment, I asked myself one simple question, "Who do you want to be, Fred?" Faced with the prospect of continuing my career in law enforcement, I couldn't shake the nagging sense that my heart wasn't fully invested in the path before me, and I had no idea why.

In a bid for some sense of normalcy, I pursued employment with a national security company, a choice born out of necessity rather than passion. Though far removed from what I perceived as a previous profession of honor, my current choice would pay the bills and be a springboard to a career with a purpose. In the meantime, it paid the bills.

In the warmth of my mother's apartment and the comfort of my mother and brother's presence, I found fleeting moments of solace from my inner demons. Gathered in the living room, we shared laughter and fond memories, reminiscing about my father and the void his absence had left in our lives. Yet, despite the semblance of normalcy that enveloped us, a deep-seated longing continued to tug at my soul, a yearning for the daughter I had left behind.

On my days off from my security job, I became a 'regular' in the familiar space of karaoke bars, accompanied by my brother in a desperate bid to drown out self-pity with our favorite bourbons. Back in familiar surroundings where I could detach from my past and responsibilities, I was once again the man with the mic. Strangers applauded and hailed me as a star. Applause and handshakes greeted me as I stepped off the stage, a fleeting moment of validation amidst the relentless self-doubt that plagued my every waking moment.

Yet, as the night wore on and the echoes of laughter faded into the silence of the early morning hours, the demons continued to stir, their mocking laughter forever in my mind. They whispered tales of inadequacy and failure, taunting me for daring to seek happiness. In the depths of my solitude, torn between the warmth of family in Delaware and the ache of separation from my daughter in Florida, I grappled with a decision that would shape my life once again. Every call to my daughter echoed with bittersweet longing, a reminder of the void that ate at my soul in the absence of her presence. Despite the comfort of my mother and brother, the ache of separation weighed heavy upon my heart, a constant reminder of the love I wanted to share with my daughter, the father I wanted to be.

I was conflicted. I appreciated the support from my family in Delaware, but it clashed with the unrelenting tug of paternal love, drawing me back to Florida. In the end, I resolved to return to Florida in the embrace of my daughter and the love that bound us together. With a heavy heart, I reached out to the jail, my former employer, swallowing my pride as I sought to reclaim the life I had left behind.

The phone call trembled in my hand; each ring seemed like an eternity. In the back of my mind, I harbored a fleeting hope that no one would answer, sparing me the shame of my return. Yet fate had other plans, as the voice on the other end ushered me into a conversation that would alter the course of my destiny. Without hesitation, the Major welcomed me home; I heard the faint strains of "Midnight Train to Georgia," a reminder of the journey ahead.

It had been only six weeks, but I bid farewell to my family and the biting cold of Delaware's winter; it was bittersweet getting on the train for my trip back to Florida. I sensed the disappointment in my mother's eyes and the understanding in my brother's embrace, yet their silent support spoke volumes. With a heavy heart and a sense of purpose, I boarded the train bound for Florida, determined to confront the demons that haunted my soul and forge a permanent path toward redemption and peace.

Starting over Again

Welcomed back with open arms, I returned to the familiar embrace of the jail, slipping seamlessly into the rhythm of care, custody, and control. I threw myself into my work, channeling my energy into the pursuit of distraction. I soon developed a reputation as the 'king of overtime.'

After leaving the confines of the jail, a new routine consisted of co-workers and me heading to restaurants to break bread together after shift; I renewed friendships deepened over trips to the bowling alley and post-shift workouts in the gym. Together, we navigated the challenges of our profession; I had a great support system of seasoned officers and those who had newly arrived with little to no experience. We grew as a family in each other's company and shared experiences. I was back with my tribe; things would be different this time.

Yet, even with the camaraderie and routine, my demons still took up residence within me. They never told me what they wanted, only reminded me that I was not worthy of happiness. The demons kept assuring me that distractions were only temporary reprieves and they would always be around. They whispered that ignoring them would not make them disappear, yet I clung to the hope that someday they would lose their grip and fade into oblivion.

The honorable profession of Corrections had become both a sanctuary and a battleground for my soul. Within the jail, I continued to find moments of peace. I had a purpose as a corrections officer. I had co-workers who cared about me. Yet, as the days wore on, I wondered, "What else is there?"

The weight of my struggles compounded the challenges of my profession, casting a shadow over my sense of purpose. The relentless stress of navigating custody disputes with my ex-wife, coupled with the ache of longing for my daughter during every parting moment, overwhelmed me.

I firmly believe the Universe sends us guidance when we listen. My guidance came in the form of a deputy who shared news of a dedicated position within the sheriff's office previously unknown to me. The position of 'School Resource Deputy' offered a chance to make a meaningful impact on the lives of young people and be a guiding light in their journey through adolescence. The journey would require me to attend the law enforcement academy while maintaining my full-time position at the jail—a daunting task that I embraced with determination.

With the Major's blessing, I started transitioning from a corrections officer to a deputy sheriff. Through grit and determination, I (again) navigated the rigors of training, emerging with hope and a new beginning. I completed the academy and passed the state test.

As I stood before the Major and thanked him for the opportunity to serve as a corrections officer, I was ready to begin my new career. Since the county jail and the sheriff's office were both under the sheriff's jurisdiction, the major escorted me to an interview with a panel of sheriff's office administrators to become a deputy sheriff. My Major sat beside me, and I felt a sense of pride when he explained to the panel that he was sorry to see me leave the jail but was confident that I would be an asset as a deputy sheriff. The Major then spoke of my strong communication skills and my commitment to duty. That day, I remember feeling immense pride as I listened to affidavits sent in to be read before the panel from former peers and superiors who had previously worked with me.

Do you acknowledge and commend the people under your command? When was the last time you told someone you appreciated their hard work?

Deputy Sheriff

Navigating the transition from corrections officer to deputy sheriff was an uncertain journey. In addition to the rigorous training I received at the academy, I was also required to serve two years on Road Patrol before being assigned to a school. Nothing could have prepared me for the realities of life on the road. The Florida Statute Book was a daunting thousand (plus) page challenge, its intricacies requiring a deep understanding to navigate the complexities of law enforcement.

Confidence became my most prized asset in this new role. There were moments of hesitation, times when I sought reassurance from my zone partners, ensuring that a firm grasp of the law backed every arrest. I grew more proficient and more confident in my ability to uphold the law and serve my community with dedication with each day served.

I patrolled the streets. I embraced being mentored. I looked forward to guiding those who would follow in my footsteps. I enjoyed the camaraderie and sense of purpose of patrolling my zone; However, a stark reality emerged—a departure from the glamorized portrayal of law enforcement. Contrary to popular belief, the life of a law enforcement officer was not car chases and shootouts. Instead, it was a meticulous dance of paperwork, courtroom proceedings, and more paperwork.

Even with Hollywood's picture being far from the truth, the mundane tasks and bureaucratic hurdles provided a sense of purpose. I was steadfastly committed to upholding the law and safeguarding the communities we swore to protect.

Transitioning from the structured environment of corrections to the dynamic world of road patrol was a profound shift in my law enforcement journey. Under the guidance of three different field training officers, I relentlessly pursued proficiency, striving to meet the rigorous standards necessary to earn my zone. Each day on the road was an eye-opening revelation, a stark reminder that law enforcement is not about responding to people having a good day but rather to those engulfed in crisis.

With nearly three decades of experience in law enforcement and corrections, I am continually astonished by the prevalence of perpetual crisis in the lives of so many individuals. It is a sobering realization that crisis has become an accepted norm for some—a harsh reality that defies conventional understanding.

During my tenure on road patrol, I delved into the intricacies of my Florida Statute manual, honing my skills to navigate the complexities of the law. I would soon realize that it was not the technical or legal frameworks, but the human element that resonated most deeply. Serving and protecting transcended mere enforcement—it was about providing solace and support in times of distress. Whether apprehending an abusive spouse or connecting individuals with vital social services, every action felt like a tangible contribution to the betterment of society.

However, the emotional toll of law enforcement proved to be an unforeseen challenge. Each call brought with it a whirlwind of emotions, from the heart-wrenching search for a lost elderly person to the adrenaline-fueled chaos of an armed home invasion. The constant cycle of crisis left me emotionally drained after every shift, grappling with the weight of human suffering and uncertainty.

The rotation of shifts added another layer of complexity to my experience. The grueling schedule, alternating between day and night shifts every four months, took a toll on both body and mind. Nights, in particular, became a dreaded ordeal and battle of fatigue.

Through it all, my commitment to serving the community endured. Despite the challenges and sacrifices, I wanted to impact people's lives. It was during this period that I started to understand the concept of gratitude. It doesn't find you; you have to seek it.

One afternoon in the middle of my shift, I received the call to report to the road patrol office. A familiar sense of unease settled over me once again. The anticipation of what awaited me returned the negative talk inside my head. A mounting sense of dread weighed down each step toward the supervisor's office. It was a well-known fact that being summoned to the office mid-shift rarely spelled good news. More often than not, it signaled a reprimand or, worse yet, a trip to the dreaded Internal Affairs office.

With each passing moment, my heart raced faster, the rhythmic pounding echoing in my ears as I ascended the stairs to the second floor. My mind raced, grappling with the possibilities of what could have prompted this summons. Had someone filed a complaint against me? Was I about to face disciplinary action?

As I entered the supervisor's office, the tension in the air was thick with anticipation. Taking my seat in front of his desk, I braced myself for the inevitable blow. The only positive message to myself was that at least I had completed my probation period; they couldn't fire me without cause. With a single sentence, the course of my career was placed on a new path.

"You are being transferred to the School Resource Unit," the supervisor announced, his words ringing out with a finality; it happened quicker than I anticipated, but those words were welcoming. Once again, I would leave a shift I had grown fond of. Total strangers became friends. I truly understood what people meant when they spoke of a brotherhood. People that you barely know would give their life for you. I finally understood what existed behind the badge.

School is In Session

Being transferred to the School Resource Unit was a pivotal moment in my career, one that carried with it a weight of anticipation. In the law enforcement community, such a move could be viewed through various lenses, each tinted with its shade of perception. Some may see it as a form of punishment, relegating deputies deemed unfit for street duty to the confines of a school setting. Others might perceive school resource officers as little more than glorified babysitters resigned to a role of retirement in place.

However, I refused to be defined by these narrow stereotypes. For me, the role of a School Resource Deputy was not merely a job assignment but a profound calling. It resonated with me on a deeply personal level, drawing upon my upbringing and the invaluable guidance and discipline instilled by my parents. Their support had seen me through the darkest of times, and now, I was determined to pay it forward.

Unlike many of my students, I had the privilege of growing up in a stable household with both parents present. Yet, as I explored my role as a School Resource Deputy, I faced the harsh reality that not all students were as fortunate. Many grappled with challenges far beyond their years, navigating tumultuous waters without parental guidance.

It was within the realm of the School Resource Unit that I found my true purpose: bridging the gap between law enforcement and the community by providing mentorship, guidance, and support to students in need. It was because of this role that I completed the cross-over course from corrections to law enforcement, solidifying my commitment to serving and protecting those in our community who needed it most: our children.

As I honed my skills as a School Resource Deputy, I encountered the stark reality of the challenges facing many families in our community. Single-parent households were common, and I witnessed firsthand the immense burden placed on those shouldering the responsibility of provider and disciplinarian.

In meetings, I witnessed the strain and exhaustion etched into the faces of single parents as they dealt with the myriad of responsibilities thrust upon them. The weight of being the sole provider and disciplinarian and wearing countless other hats took its toll, often leaving parents at their breaking point. I watched as they struggled to maintain control of their children, with some reaching a moment of desperation where blame was cast upon the school or law enforcement rather than addressing the root of the child's behavior.

Tragically, I also witnessed the heart-wrenching loss of students in accidents, students who died in watercraft, or, far more common, car accidents. I endured the task of apprehending students for committing acts of violence or bringing weapons onto campus, a duty that weighed heavily on my heart. Escorting students to receiving centers for mental health evaluations and listening to their cries of hopelessness from the back seat of my patrol car underscored the dire need for intervention and support in their lives.

Despite the challenges, working in the schools allowed me to develop meaningful relationships with students and families. I was initially taken aback by the number of students who harbored distrust or outright animosity towards me as a law enforcement, particularly as a black male who understood what they were going through and was there for them. I recognized that much of this sentiment stemmed from learned behavior. Yet, I couldn't help but question the role they experienced in past encounters with law enforcement outside the school setting, especially among the high school students I engaged with.

I gained a deeper understanding of the complex interplay between trauma, community dynamics, and law enforcement interactions. It fueled my passion for fostering empathy and bridging the divide between law enforcement and the community, particularly among those who may harbor deep-seated distrust or negative perceptions.

Within the school campus, I was drawn to the students undergoing identity crises, particularly those transitioning from middle to high school. Among them, the freshmen often struggled the most to find their place, their behavior betraying their inner turmoil and the masks they wore to conceal their insecurities. Some displayed signs of being lost souls crying out for help, while others sought to cover up various perceived 'deficits' from the world. I distinctly remember this time in my own life and I believe it made me a better School Resource Deputy.

Navigating the delicate balance between school policy violations and potential violations of state statutes was a constant challenge. I was acutely aware of the repercussions that could follow a trip to jail for a young person. The gravity of the situation was not lost on me. I was careful to consider each decision, ever-mindful of the potential long-term impact on their lives.

There were moments of profound reward. Wearing the dual hats of law enforcement officer and mentor allowed me to make a tangible difference in students' lives. I vividly remember the astonishment of students as they entered the cafeteria for their after-school dance, only to find me standing on stage in full uniform, ready to DJ their event. Their disbelief quickly turned to admiration and awe as they rushed to the stage, their eyes filled with wonder and excitement at the unexpected sight before them.

These moments of connection and impact reinforced my commitment to fostering positive relationships and providing support to students in need, even as I grappled with the complexities and challenges inherent in my role as a School Resource Deputy. As I stood on stage, spinning tunes and connecting with students through the universal language of music, I encountered a diverse array of reactions. Some students, too cool to approach the stage or harboring a deep-seated aversion to law enforcement officers, remained aloof. Yet, over the years, whether in elementary, middle, or high school, I found ways to break down those barriers and win many of them over.

Music became my tool for bridging divides and revealing the humanity behind the badge. It provided a platform for meaningful interactions, allowing me to connect with students from different backgrounds and foster a deeper understanding and respect. Through music, I was able to show them that law enforcement officers were more than just authority figures – we were individuals with stories, emotions, and a genuine desire to make a positive impact.

My time in the schools was undeniably rewarding. I had the privilege of meeting hundreds, if not thousands, of students throughout my assignments. Many of their parents became my friends, and our bonds have endured. Watching these students, whom I affectionately called "my kids," grow into responsible adults brought me immense pride. Some pursued higher education or vocational training, becoming productive members of society. Others, sadly struggled with negative behaviors that persisted into adulthood, leading to encounters with the law. Encounters that often brought them back into my orbit, this time as inmates in the jail where I worked overtime.

Through it all, the power of music remained a constant thread, weaving its way through my interactions with students and shaping the connections I forged with them and their families. It was a reminder of the permanent impact we can have when we approach our roles with empathy, understanding, and a willingness to engage with those we serve on a deeper level.

In 2006, I decided to step away from my role in the schools and venture into the challenging world as a narcotics detective. I was honored to serve my community in this capacity, the pride in playing a part in combatting the devastating impact of drugs on our neighborhoods, was undeniable. Having witnessed firsthand how drugs had ravaged my community growing up. Drug trafficking leaves behind a devastating trail of destruction, and I was determined to do my part in "cleaning up the streets."

My time in the drug unit was intense and eye-opening. I immersed myself in building cases and making arrests, confronting the grim reality of the drug trade and its consequences. It was a world where human life seemed expendable, where violence and disregard for the sanctity of life were disturbingly commonplace. I asked the profound questions: How do they live with themselves? How do people transform into individuals who once valued life but now have succumbed to a life devoid of empathy and compassion?

The experiences I encountered during my stint in the drug unit left an indelible mark on me. While I recognized the importance of combating drug-related crime, I realized that my true calling was to return to the schools, engaging students before they reached a point of no return. I was driven by a deep-seated passion to make a difference in the lives of young people and to intervene before they fell victim to the lure of drugs and violence.

My decision to leave the drug unit was a choice rooted in my belief that prevention and intervention were vital in addressing the underlying issues that fueled the cycle of drug abuse and crime. Returning to the schools allowed me to pursue my mission of reaching out to students and guiding them away from the destructive paths that awaited them if left unchecked.

Reflecting on my journey, I am reminded of the importance of empathy and understanding in law enforcement. The experiences I encountered, the trauma I witnessed, reinforced my commitment to bridging the gap between law enforcement and the community. My goal has always been to foster a deeper understanding and compassion among officers and those they serve, to create a safer, more supportive environment for all.

D.A.R.E

Prior to departing from the narcotics unit, I received an unexpected call from my friend Terry. His warm congratulations on my decision to return to the schools and follow my heart were a welcome reassurance. But what caught me off guard was his invitation to join the D.A.R.E.

program – an opportunity he described as even more fulfilling than my current path.

The D.A.R.E. program, Drug Abuse Resistance and Education, had been established years prior in Los Angeles. Its mission was clear: to educate and empower students with essential life skills and decision-making tools to resist drugs and other harmful substances. At the time, our sheriff's office boasted a dedicated D.A.R.E. unit comprising six deputies who covered over 20 elementary schools in our county.

Eager to make a meaningful impact, I applied for the position within the D.A.R.E Unit and was thrilled to be selected. Little did I know it would become one of the most fulfilling roles of my law enforcement career.

Walking into those elementary school classrooms each week filled me with anticipation. The students' eager faces, hanging on to every word I spoke, reminded me of the profound influence law enforcement officers can have as positive role models. For many of these children, I realized I might be the only male figure offering guidance and support in their lives.

I endeavored to go beyond the curriculum in each lesson, spending extra time with students who needed it most. Whether offering encouragement, listening to their concerns, or simply being a consistent presence, I cherished every opportunity to make a difference in their lives.

The D.A.R.E. program provided invaluable education to students and served as a bridge between law enforcement and communities that often felt marginalized. Seeing officers in a different light was transformative for students from disadvantaged backgrounds. Likewise, it offered parents from those same communities a chance to witness law enforcement officers in a positive and nurturing role during D.A.R.E. graduations.

During my tenure with the D.A.R.E. Unit, I forged lasting bonds with school staff and witnessed the growth of countless students as they navigated through the education system. Many of them made commendable choices and even went on to join our agency, a testament to the program's impact.

However, like many cherished initiatives, the D.A.R.E. unit eventually faced an unfortunate end. In the wake of the 2008 housing crisis, nationwide budget cuts became inevitable across law enforcement agencies, including ours. As a result, the difficult decision was made to disband the unit to avoid layoffs, with some deputies returning to full-time school assignments (like me) while others were reassigned to road patrol duties.

Amidst these professional changes, 2009 marked a significant personal milestone as I met the love of my life. A School Psychologist by profession, she shared my passion for serving the community through education. Our connection had been years in the making, though circumstances had previously kept us apart. It wasn't until later, after her previous marriage had ended that we found ourselves drawn to each other more profoundly.

My wife guided my journey towards becoming a better man, husband, and officer. Her steadfast support and insight would prove invaluable as I continued to navigate the complexities of law enforcement while striving to address the emotional toll it often took.

During my time at Leesburg High School (I felt compelled to shout out), one of the busiest schools in the county, I encountered a stark contrast between perception and reality. Mentioning the school's name often elicited responses like, "Wow, I heard that was the worst school high school." Yet, this perception couldn't have been further from the truth. While the school had its share of challenges, including frequent fights, it also housed students from underprivileged communities striving to break barriers.

Behind the facade of turmoil lay stories of resilience and determination. Despite the chaos, students from the same neighborhoods were pursuing certifications as nursing assistants and participating in construction classes. At one point, the school boasted more National Honor Society students than any other in the county. It was a reminder not to judge a book by its cover, to see beyond the collective surface and recognize the individual potential within.

On the Road Again

In 2013, I received a promotion to Corporal, which came with excitement and apprehension. I questioned if I was prepared to become a front-line supervisor; the initial plan was to keep me in the schools as a supervisor. However, I surprised the Sheriff by requesting to return to the road. It was a decision that caught him off guard, as he knew how deeply I cherished my time in the schools and the impact I strived to make on the students during my nearly decade-long tenure in the school resource unit. But I knew in order to grow as a supervisor I would need to be uncomfortable, back on the road as a supervisor where I would have to develop and relearn skills.

As I prepared to transition back to the road patrol unit, a sense of loneliness crept over me. My dedication to protecting the county's youth has been my calling for nearly a decade. Was I abandoning that calling by leaving? Deep down, I knew that my connection with youth would always be a part of me. Pursuing one's passion transcends physical locations; it's ingrained in one's being. And so, armed with my experiences, I prepared to bring my passion for service to the road patrol unit, ready to face whatever challenges lay ahead.

Stepping back onto the road as a supervisor was daunting. I was about to lead a group of officers, some of whom had more road patrol experience than I had. It had been years since I'd been on road patrol full-time, and I worried that some might view my promotion as an affirmative action move, which couldn't have been further from the truth.

My journey to becoming a Corporal wasn't without its challenges. I had taken the Corporal exam twice before. I didn't adequately prepare the first time and failed the written exam, preventing me from advancing to the oral board, which was typically my strong suit. Determined to succeed, I retook the exam and scored the minimum eighty percent required to move on to the oral boards, yet I was still unsuccessful in promotion. However, my third attempt at the exam coincided with a nine-day trip my wife and I took to Jamaica. Despite being in one of my favorite Caribbean destinations, I remained committed to my goal, dedicating three hours each day to study surrounded by the serenity of the island.

My game plan worked flawlessly. I scored an impressive 90 on the written exam and soared into the top five during the intense oral board assessment. It took some time, but eventually, I earned the promotion I had worked so hard for. I vividly recall the day of the promotional ceremony, scanning the audience and locking eyes with my mother. The pride radiating from her was palpable, a moment etched into my memory for eternity.

And so, with my promotion secured, the real work began. I transitioned from the familiar routine of waking up at 5 am for nearly a decade to embarking on a shift that commenced at 6 pm and stretched until 6 am the following morning. Lake County sprawls across a vast expanse of 1100 square miles, and I often found myself driving an hour each way to reach the sector where I served as supervisor. The rotation was relentless, with four months of night shift followed by four months of day shift, and then the cycle was repeated once more.

My Sergeant, though about ten years my junior, possessed a wealth of experience on the road and in supervision. He welcomed me aboard with open arms and encouraged me to sit back and absorb the ebb and flow of radio traffic. As I grew accustomed to the rhythm of operations and learned to allocate resources efficiently while prioritizing calls for service, I gradually eased into my role.

It didn't take long for me to find my footing. I've always had a keen ear and a natural talent for effective communication. While I certainly didn't have all the answers, I approached my new role humbly, acknowledging that I still had much to learn. What I did possess, however, was a genuine care for those under my supervision and a sincere desire to see them succeed. In the early days of my supervisory journey, if I ever faltered on a call or overlooked requesting a necessary resource, my seasoned colleagues would discreetly offer guidance via text message. Their support was invaluable, and they never once made me feel inadequate in my role.

Returning to road patrol was a stark reminder of the darkness that lurked within humanity. It was a sobering realization of the pain and hopelessness many individuals grappled with daily. I gained a newfound appreciation for the resilience of my colleagues in the road patrol unit, who confronted these challenges head-on, day in and day out.

In law enforcement, we confront the raw pain and trauma of those we serve, often on an hourly basis. We are expected to find solutions to deep-seated societal problems that have plagued communities for decades if not centuries. However, my time back on road patrol reaffirmed that the tools at our disposal are merely band-aids, offering temporary relief but unable to address the root causes of societal ills.

Despite these limitations, my role as a supervisor on road patrol was gratifying. While we may not have had all the answers, I believe we provided a semblance of relief to many of our citizens, if only momentarily. Whether it was apprehending an abusive spouse or a homicide suspect, reuniting a lost autistic child with their family, or an elderly dementia patient with their spouse, each success was a testament to the impact we could have, even in the midst of chaos.

Reflecting on this chapter of my career, I realized the fleeting nature of these moments of success. In the whirlwind of crisis management, there was barely a moment to savor the victories before diving headfirst into the next emergency.

After a year as a Corporal on road patrol, the following promotional exam loomed. I once again dedicated myself to rigorous study and preparation, determined to seize the opportunity for advancement. When the exam day arrived, I performed admirably, landing in the top ten candidates. It seemed my path was set to continue as a sergeant on road patrol, a prospect I welcomed eagerly.

However, fate had other plans in store for me.

Back in my teenage years, I found solace and purpose on the stage. As a member of the Gainesville Area Improvisational Teen Theater, I delved into the world of performance, tackling skits that explored pressing issues like teen pregnancy, bullying, and suicide—those formative years laid the groundwork for my love of storytelling and communication.

As I transitioned into my twenties, I continued to nurture my passion for acting through community theater. The stage became my sanctuary, a place where I could express myself and connect with others. Whether embodying a character or delivering a monologue, I thrived in the spotlight, relishing every moment of shared emotion and vulnerability.

Fast forward to 2014, a pivotal moment in my life and career. I was on the cusp of a significant promotion to Sergeant when I received an unexpected summons to the sheriff's office. The mere mention of meeting the sheriff sent a jolt of apprehension through me, igniting a whirlwind of thoughts and emotions as I made my way to his office.

Throughout my journey in law enforcement, the sheriff had been more than just a superior – he was a mentor and a guiding light. Under his leadership as a Major over the detention center, I embarked on my career back in 1997. With only nine months of experience as a correctional officer in a state prison, he took a chance on me, recognizing my potential and offering me the opportunity to grow personally and professionally.

As I stepped into the sheriff's office, gratitude and trepidation consumed me. The weight of anticipation hung heavy as I awaited his words. Reflecting on our shared history, I felt deeply indebted to him for the faith he had shown me.

Highs and lows, triumphs and challenges have marked my journey through law enforcement. Along the way, I've come to understand the profound impact that trauma can have on those in the profession. As a certified emotional intelligence trainer, I aimed to bridge the gap between law enforcement and the community, fostering understanding and empathy on both sides.

As I sat across from the sheriff in his office, a wave of relief washed over me when I saw the smile on his face. It was a stark contrast to the anxiety that had gripped me moments before. We engaged in small talk for a few minutes, easing into the conversation before he dropped a bombshell of a question that caught me entirely off guard.

"How would you like to be one of my public information officers?" The words hung in the air, and I struggled to process the unexpected proposition. The weight of the responsibility and the magnitude of what he offered me settled heavily on my shoulders. The role demanded dedication, availability, and poise, traits I knew I possessed but had never envisioned channeling in this particular capacity.

As the sheriff elaborated on the role, outlining the demands and expectations, I couldn't help but feel a surge of excitement mingled with apprehension. The thought of stepping into the spotlight as a spokesperson for our agency, representing myself and my community, ignited a fire within me. It was an opportunity to defy expectations, to challenge stereotypes, and to carve out a space where I could make a difference.

I left the sheriff's office that day with a whirlwind of emotions swirling inside me. The prospect of becoming a public information officer was daunting, but it was also a chance to prove my worth to the agency and myself. I returned home to discuss the offer with my wife, knowing deep down that this was an opportunity I couldn't pass up.

As I embarked on training for the role, shadowing my lieutenant as he prepared stories for public consumption, I quickly realized the gravity of the task. It wasn't simply about relaying information but about telling the story in its entirety, capturing the nuances and complexities beneath the surface.

The importance of accuracy and empathy became clear as I delved into the narratives behind arrests and incidents. It wasn't enough to recite the facts from an arrest affidavit; I had to delve deeper to uncover the human stories behind the headlines. This realization was sobering, a reminder of the weight of the responsibility I had undertaken.

But amidst the challenges and uncertainties, an undeniable sense of purpose drove me forward. I was determined to do justice to the stories I shared, to honor the lives and experiences of those involved, and to bridge the gap between law enforcement and the community through honest and compassionate communication. It was a journey fraught with obstacles and setbacks but also fueled by passion, determination, and a commitment to making a difference.

Navigating my role as a public information officer demanded focus and a delicate balance between transparency and discretion. With each new piece of information, I walked a tightrope, carefully weighing the need for disclosure against the potential negative impact on ongoing investigations.

One of the most significant challenges I encountered was the necessity to redact or amend reports as new details emerged or inaccuracies came to light. This was a humbling experience, requiring me to set aside my ego and prioritize accuracy above all else. It also reminded me of the importance of humility and accountability in my position.

Transparency was a core value of our agency, but it was not without its challenges. There were moments when I had to withhold particular details, particularly in sensitive cases like homicide investigations, where divulging too much could jeopardize the work of our detectives. It was a delicate dance that required me to navigate the fine line between providing the public with the information they deserved and safeguarding the integrity of our investigations.

While facing these challenges, I discovered the power of relationships. Building strong connections with my colleagues in various departments within the agency was invaluable, enabling me to access accurate information swiftly and efficiently. Whether collaborating with road patrol supervisors, liaising with detectives, or coordinating with the communication center and evidence bureau, these relationships were the lifeblood of my role.

However, perhaps most crucial were the relationships forged with media members. In an age where information spreads quickly, cultivating trust and rapport with journalists had become paramount. There were instances when the media would uncover incidents before I was even aware of them, underscoring the importance of maintaining open lines of communication and being proactive in my interactions with the press.

HowExpert Presents

How to Jump Higher

Your Step By Step Guide To Jump Higher

HowExpert

For more tips related to this topic, visit HowExpert.com/jump.

Recommended Resources

- HowExpert.com – Quick 'How To' Guides on All Topics from A to Z by Everyday Experts.
- HowExpert.com/free – Free HowExpert Email Newsletter.
- HowExpert.com/books – HowExpert Books
- HowExpert.com/courses – HowExpert Courses
- HowExpert.com/clothing – HowExpert Clothing
- HowExpert.com/membership – HowExpert Membership Site
- HowExpert.com/affiliates – HowExpert Affiliate Program
- HowExpert.com/writers – Write About Your #1 Passion/Knowledge/Expertise & Become a HowExpert Author.
- HowExpert.com/resources – Additional HowExpert Recommended Resources
- YouTube.com/HowExpert – Subscribe to HowExpert YouTube.
- Instagram.com/HowExpert – Follow HowExpert on Instagram.
- Facebook.com/HowExpert – Follow HowExpert on Facebook.

Publisher's Foreword

Dear HowExpert reader,

HowExpert publishes quick 'how to' guides on all topics from A to Z by everyday experts.

At HowExpert, our mission is to discover, empower, and maximize talents of everyday people to ultimately make a positive impact in the world for all topics from A to Z...one everyday expert at a time!

All of our HowExpert guides are written by everyday people just like you and me who have a passion, knowledge, and expertise for a specific topic.

We take great pride in selecting everyday experts who have a passion, great writing skills, and knowledge about a topic that they love to be able to teach you about the topic you are also passionate about and eager to learn about.

We hope you get a lot of value from our HowExpert guides and it can make a positive impact in your life in some kind of way. All of our readers including you altogether help us continue living our mission of making a positive impact in the world for all spheres of influences from A to Z.

If you enjoyed one of our HowExpert guides, then please take a moment to send us your feedback from wherever you got this book.

Thank you and we wish you all the best in all aspects of life.

Sincerely,

BJ Min
Founder & Publisher of HowExpert
HowExpert.com

PS...If you are also interested in becoming a HowExpert author, then please visit our website at HowExpert.com/writers. Thank you & again, all the best!

COPYRIGHT, LEGAL NOTICE AND DISCLAIMER:

Table of Contents

Introduction

There are a lot of sports and other athletic activities that require athletes to be able to jump very high. Whether you play basketball, jump hurdles, or volleyball, you know the importance of being able to jump high.

You might think it's impossible to jump higher than you already do, but chances are you're wrong. In fact, there are steps you can take to increase your jumping height significantly. This eBook will show you seven steps to jumping higher, and improving your athletic ability.

Following these steps will do more than just teach you to jump higher; you will also learn to improve your overall level of fitness in the process.

Step 1: Improve Your Overall Fitness

One key factor in how high you can jump is your weight. By taking steps to improve your overall fitness, you'll lose weight, and consequently you'll be able to jump higher.

There are two key factors in improving your overall fitness: diet and exercise.

By making a few simple changes to both your diet and your exercise routine, you can lose down to your ideal weight, and increase your jumping height.

Start by adjusting your diet.

Try to cut out any junk food that might still be a part of your diet, and cut down on carbs and fatty foods. Even just cutting down the size of the portions you eat at each meal can have a dramatic impact on your weight over time. You might be surprised at just how much weight you can lose just by making a few simple tweaks to your diet.

If you're looking for something a little more regimented, there are a number of structured diets available to you. Just search the internet for a diet that suits your needs, and start shedding the pounds.

There are two ways to start a new diet. You can either jump right into it, or you can ease your way in. If you want to jump straight into your diet, start by getting rid of all of the food in your house that doesn't fit your new diet. Then, take a trip to the grocery store, and buy some new groceries that fit with your new diet.

Easing into your new diet works a little different. Start by making small changes to the portions you eat, and the types of foods you include in each meal. If you make a few small changes each week, after a little while, your diet will be going strong.

The other essential component in weight loss is exercise.

If you're already on an exercise regime, you can make some significant progress with your weight loss by adding a little extra cardio to your workout schedule. Try running for a half hour four times a week in addition to your existing workout schedule. You'll be surprised at the difference it makes.

How to Improve Your Overall Fitness

- Get in better shape; the more physically fit you are, the higher you will be able to jump without the extra weight.
- Improve your diet through eating more vegetables and fruit and reducing junk food to the bare minimum.
- Step up your exercise routine. Jumping and power lower body movements should be your focus.

Step 2: Targeted Exercises

There are a lot of exercises designed specifically to work your legs and help you to jump higher. Either add these exercises to your workout, or start a new workout regime focused around them if you want to jump higher. When doing each of the following exercises, focus on the number of reps rather than adding weight.

Squats are one of the best exercises for increasing your leg strength, and improving your vertical leap. Squats can either be done in a squat rack with weight, or anywhere that you have enough space to do them.

To do a squat, start in a standing position with your legs somewhat spread. Begin by bending at the knees, keeping your back straight and your knees above with your feet. Once you reach the point where your knees make a ninety-degree angle, begin to rise back up.

How to Do Squats To Jump Higher:

- Legs shoulder width apart.
- Squat down to no more than 90 degrees.
- Inhale on way down, exhale on way up.
- Keep back flexed and straight.

Lunges are another great exercise to help you increase your vertical leap. Lunges help to build up the muscles in your quads, and they can be done with, or without, weights.

To do a lunge, start in a standing position, and lunge forward with one leg until that leg's knee is at a ninety-degree angle. Slide back to a standing position, and repeat the process with your other leg. The whole time you're doing the lunges, you have to keep your torso straight.

How to Do Lunges To Jump Higher:

- Stand straight up, legs close together.
- Step forward with one leg, bend knee straight down.
- Keep back straight and flexed.
- Do not exceed a 90-degree angle on front leg.
- Stand back to straight (push back with front leg), repeat with other leg.

Toe raises can help you to increase your vertical leap by strengthening your calf muscles. You can either use a toe raise machine in a gym, or even use a thick piece of wood at home.

How to Do Toe Raises to Jump Higher:

- Start with your heel hanging off the edge, and raise up onto your tippy toes.
- Then, just lower yourself back down, and repeat the process.

Step ups will also help to improve your vertical leap by working many of the muscles in your legs.

How to Do Step Ups to Jump Higher:

- Find a low chair or bench, and step up onto it with your right foot.
- Step back down, and then repeat the process, except this time, lead in with your left foot.
- Continue in that fashion.

So, your workout should include the following exercises to help you improve your vertical leap:

- Squats
- Lunges
- Toe Raises
- Step Ups

All four of these exercises will help you to jump higher. If they're not already a part of your workout, incorporate them into your exercise regime.

If they are already a part of your workout, consider using weights while you do these exercises to help increase their effectiveness.

Step 3: Plyometrics

Another type of exercise essential to increasing your vertical leap is plyometrics. Plyometrics is a type of exercise designed to generate fast and powerful movements in your muscles.

If you're going to make plyometrics a part of your workout, it's absolutely essential that you take the time to do a proper warm up.

Take the time to stretch, and then either do some jogging, or run up and down the steps a few times. Plyometrics can be an intense workout, so warming up, and getting your muscles ready for the workout they're about to get is essential.

The three plyometrics exercises to help you jump higher fast are deep knee jumps, jump roping, and fast skips.

How to Do Deep Knee Jumps to Jump Higher:

- Deep knee jumps are one type of plyometrics exercise that will greatly help to improve your vertical leap.
- Doing a deep knee jump is similar to a squat, except that you want to move down toward the ground a little quicker, and once your bottom is almost touching the ground, leap up as high as possible.

- Once your feet are back on the ground, immediately start going back down toward the ground.
- Start by doing 15 of these at a time, and work your way up to 20, and eventually 30 or more.

How to Jump Rope to Jump Higher:

- Jumping rope is another plyometrics exercise that will help you to increase your jump height.
    - Spend at least fifteen minutes a day jumping rope at a nice quick pace.
    - It's a good idea to watch TV or listen to the radio while jumping rope if you can – doing so will help to pass the time, and you'll be getting a great workout without even realizing it.

How to Do Fast Skips to Jump Higher:

- Fast skips will also help you to improve your vertical leap.
- Fast skips are just like regular skipping, except, well, faster.
    - Fast skipping for 25 minutes a day, three days a week will result in explosive power in your jumps.

So, to recap, your workout should include the following plyometrics which will help you increase your jump height.

- Deep Knee Jumps
- Jump Roping
- Fast Skips

Plyometrics can be very physically demanding, and as such, it's important to exercise appropriate caution when doing them.

Athletes under the age of 13, and athletes over 240 pounds should stick to a low volume of plyometrics exercises. Whenever possible, perform plyometrics exercises on a soft surface like a gymnastics mat.

If you have any sort of heart or respiratory condition, consult a physician before making plyometrics part of your workout.

Step 4: Stretching

The flexibility in your legs is directly related to the amount of power they can generate.

By taking the appropriate steps to improve your flexibility, you'll also be working to improve the power you can put behind your jump, and ultimately, you'll improve your vertical leap. By using the right stretches, you can easily increase both your flexibility and power.

You'll want to stretch the following muscles in order to improve your vertical leap:

- Quadriceps
- Calves
- Hamstrings

How to Stretch Your Quadriceps to Jump Higher

In order to stretch your quadriceps, there's a particular type of kneeling stretch you should use.

- Start by kneeling on the ground with your back straight.
- Put one foot out in front of you so that your knee is at a ninety-degree angle, and your foot is planted on the ground in front of you.
- Reach behind you, and get a good firm grip on the foot that's behind you.

- Pull it up toward your bottom slowly until you can feel the front of your hip and thigh stretching.
- Hold that position for 20 – 30 seconds, and then slowly lower the foot down. Switch legs and repeat the process.

How to Stretch Your Calves to Jump Higher

It's also a good idea to stretch your calves.

- Find a firm surface that you can put your weight on safely, like a wall.
- Stand arm's length from that surface, and plant your hands firmly on it.
- Bend one leg forward slightly as you would in a lunge, and stretch the other leg out behind you.
- Push until you feel your calf stretching, and then hold the position for about 20 – 30 seconds, and then switch legs.

How to Stretch Your Hamstrings to Jump Higher

You're also going to want to stretch your hamstrings.

- Start from a standing position.

- Bring your feet together, but don't lock your knees.
- Reach down and touch your toes, keeping your legs straight.
- If you can't reach your toes, just reach as far down as you can until you feel the back of your thighs stretching.
- Once again, hold the position, and then slowly return to a standing position.

Making these stretches a part of your workout routine will help you to increase both the flexibility in your legs, and the power with which you jump.

Don't underestimate the usefulness of a good set of stretches when you're trying to improve your vertical leap.

Step 5: Practice Jumping

One of the best ways to increase your jumping height is simply to jump. If you incorporate some jumping exercises into your workout, the end result will be increased skill and height when jumping.

Step by Step Jump Practice:

1. **Start your jumping workout off with a five-minute warm up run.**
    - Whenever you're going to be exercising your legs, it's important to take the time to warm up first.
2. **The next step is to stretch.**
    - Try doing the stretches mentioned above before diving into your jump workout. The stretches combined with the workout will have a positive impact on your vertical leap.
3. **The first exercise you should do as a part of your jumping workout is one-legged jumps.**
    - Do three sets of ten jumps with each leg, alternating legs between sets.
    - Once you're done with your one-legged jumps, take a two-minute break.
4. **Next up, you should do ten regular (two legged) vertical jumps.**
    - After each jump, take the time to reset yourself to a normal standing position.

- Remember, this exercise isn't about how fast you can get through the jumps, but about how high up you jump.

5. **Now do ten more vertical jumps with ten-pound weights in each hand.**
    - Again, take the time to reset yourself to a normal standing position between jumps.
    - Jump as high as you can each time.
    - Again, this exercise is about how high you can jump, not how fast you can get through each jump.
6. **Ten more regular vertical jumps.**
7. **Ten more regular vertical jumps with weights.**
8. **Once you're done, run for five more minutes.**
9. **Stretch to cool down.**
    - Running and stretching to cool down are necessary to avoid muscle cramps, so make sure you take the time to do both.

So, to recap, your jumping workout will look like this:

1. Five-minute Warm Up Run
2. Stretching
3. One Legged Jumps
4. Vertical Jumps
5. Vertical Jumps with Weight
6. Vertical Jumps
7. Vertical Jumps with Weight
8. 5 Minute Cool Down Run
9. Cool Down Stretches

This workout is designed specifically to help you to improve your jumping skills. Over time, you may want to increase your reps, or maybe even your weights, though it isn't necessary to do so.

Just make sure you take the time to warm up and cool down by both stretching and running.

Remember, one of the best ways to improve your jumping skills is to do exercises that involve jumping.

This workout will do a lot to improve your vertical leap, and should be included in your workout regime if you're looking to improve your jumping power and height.

Step 6: How To Improve Your Jumping Technique

Jumping is more complicated than just pushing yourself off of the floor. There are specific techniques you should follow to get the most out of each jump.

Quick Tip:

- When starting each jump, keep your feet close together, and arch your back as you begin to bend slightly at the knees to begin the jump.
- Your jump should explode from your toes, and they should be the last thing to leave the floor.

During your sporting event of choice, you may not have the chance to use a perfect technique each time you jump, but by practicing your technique while working out, you will improve your technique during your sport of choice.

It might seem simple or unimportant, but practicing good technique can make all the difference between a low jump, and a high one. Your technique can go a long way toward improving your vertical leap.

Step 7: How to Jump Higher When It Counts

The whole reason you've been doing all of these exercises and stretches is to ensure that you'll be able to jump as high as possible when it counts.

There's a big difference between jumping during your workout, and jumping during your sport of choice. It can be easy to lose sight of your training when you have to jump during an actual sporting event, but there are some things you can do to ensure that you'll be able to jump as high as possible when it counts.

One of the most important things you can do is to stay as relaxed as possible. Granted, that may be easier said than done when you're in the middle of a sporting event, but relaxed leg muscles will yield significantly more power than tense ones. By keeping your legs loose and relaxed, you will be able to jump higher than you would otherwise.

Remember your training and do all of the things you've been practicing. If you can keep your training in mind, you'll be more likely to use proper technique, and as a result, you'll jump higher than you would otherwise.

All of the exercises you've been doing have been preparing you to jump when it counts, keep them in mind, and you'll do just fine.

While it's important to keep your training in mind, you don't want to over think things. If you focus on the steps involved in jumping rather than the actual act itself, you're more likely to trip yourself up. If you're thinking too hard about what you're doing, you're going to make more mistakes, so try to keep your head clear, and don't stress out about the individual steps of each jump.

Stay relaxed, remember your training, and don't over think it. By following those steps, you will be able to make sure your hours of training pay off when it counts.

No matter how good your vertical leap is, it won't make any difference if you can't jump high when it counts. Keep these things in mind, and you won't have to worry about that – you'll just jump high when you have to.

Conclusion

Improving your vertical leap takes a real commitment of time and effort, but you can do it. By building a strong workout geared toward improving your vertical leap, you can and will learn to jump higher.

Incorporate the exercises in this book into your workout, and you'll be on your way to a better jump height before you know it. Stick to your workout regime, and practice your technique regularly, and you'll be equipped to jump as high as possible when it counts.

No matter what sport or athletic activity you take part in, if you need to jump higher, these seven steps will get you there before you know it. It might sound like a lot of work, but stick with it, and the rewards will be worth it.

Recommended Resources

- HowExpert.com – Quick 'How To' Guides on All Topics from A to Z by Everyday Experts.
- HowExpert.com/free – Free HowExpert Email Newsletter.
- HowExpert.com/books – HowExpert Books
- HowExpert.com/courses – HowExpert Courses
- HowExpert.com/clothing – HowExpert Clothing
- HowExpert.com/membership – HowExpert Membership Site
- HowExpert.com/affiliates – HowExpert Affiliate Program
- HowExpert.com/writers – Write About Your #1 Passion/Knowledge/Expertise & Become a HowExpert Author.
- HowExpert.com/resources – Additional HowExpert Recommended Resources
- YouTube.com/HowExpert – Subscribe to HowExpert YouTube.
- Instagram.com/HowExpert – Follow HowExpert on Instagram.
- Facebook.com/HowExpert – Follow HowExpert on Facebook.

Made in the USA
Columbia, SC
23 July 2024

39168460R00015

Through it all, I remained resolute in my commitment to serving as a conduit between law enforcement and the community. Despite some challenges and occasional missteps, I took pride in my role as a public information officer, knowing that my efforts played a vital role in fostering transparency, building trust, and ultimately strengthening the bond between our agency and the community we served.

Drawing inspiration from the timeless wisdom of Spiderman comics, I was reminded of the weight of responsibility that came with my role as a public information officer. Like Peter Parker's Uncle Ben, whose words echoed in my mind, I understood that with great power came great responsibility. I was entrusted with shaping narratives and telling stories that reflected the complexities of human experience – the good, the bad, and the ugly.

In those moments in front of the camera, I felt the weight of that responsibility bearing down on me. I was not just a spokesperson for our agency; I was a guardian of truth, a custodian of public trust. This role demanded integrity, courage, and unwavering commitment to the truth.

I endured the challenges and the occasional embarrassment, there was a sense of pride in knowing that I had built positive relationships with the media. While those moments were never easy, the rapport I had cultivated with journalists also made them more human. Like me, they had a job to do; they had accountability as well, and I came to respect the work they performed. It was a testament to the power of relationships and to the importance of trust and mutual respect in navigating the complexities of my role.

Becoming a public information officer put me into a spotlight I hadn't anticipated. Suddenly, I found myself navigating a realm where every word I uttered carried weight, where the slightest misstep could have far-reaching consequences. While the attention and praise from friends and colleagues were flattering, they also constantly reminded me of the pressure I faced to get it right – to uphold the principles of transparency and accountability, even in the face of adversity.

The weight of that responsibility became even more apparent as I delved into the daily task of sending out arrest affidavits to the media. Each morning, I was confronted with a litany of tragedies – stories of injustice and pain that unfolded within the confines of our community. These were not tales of heroism or bravery; they were stories of domestic violence, of loved ones betraying each other, of families torn apart by violence and despair.

Though the media reported on the arrests, they sometimes failed to capture the human toll behind each incident. Behind every arrest affidavit lay a story of heartbreak, of lives shattered and futures uncertain. It was a sobering reminder of the power of emotions, especially when those emotions are unrestrained anger—the realities of patterns of behaviors that were often overlooked or ignored.

As a public information officer, I carried the immense weight of these tragedies, witnessing the pain and suffering plaguing our community. It was a role that demanded empathy and compassion, traits that were sometimes in short supply in today's society.

I learned that in the darkness, there was also hope – hope that by shedding light on these stories and giving voice to the voiceless, we could spark change and pave the way for a brighter future. It was a responsibility that I took to heart to honor the lives and experiences of those affected by violence and injustice.

As I reflect on the tragedies that unfold behind closed doors, I am haunted by the senseless pain inflicted within the walls we call home. It's a pain that reverberates through families, leaving behind shattered lives and broken dreams. What disturbs me most is the cyclical nature of dysfunctionality, the tragic repetition of names – victims and perpetrators alike – trapped in a relentless cycle of violence and despair.

As a public information officer, I've witnessed the aftermath of these tragedies firsthand, witnessing the toll it takes on both the victims and those tasked with responding to their cries for help. The weight of their pain is palpable, a burden that weighs heavy on the hearts of law enforcement officers who must witness the darkest moments of human existence.

I still remember the day when my pain was laid bare for the world to see when tears streamed down my face on live television. It was a moment of vulnerability, a raw display of emotion in the face of unimaginable tragedy. My lieutenant and I had responded to a call where a father had allegedly drowned his toddler daughter in a bathtub. The scene was a haunting tableau of grief and horror, and it will be etched into my memory forever.

The death of a child at the hands of a parent is a wound that never truly heals, a reminder of the fragility of life and the depths of human depravity. It's a pain that cuts to the core of our humanity, leaving us stunned that a human could commit such a brutal and senseless act.

But in this darkness, I found a platform to amplify voices, share perspectives, and bridge the divide between communities. I have been given a platform to present both the perspective of the black man and the law enforcement officer and to highlight our shared humanity despite our differences.

The challenge lies in our willingness to come together, sit at the same table, and confront the uncomfortable truths that divide us. It demands courage and empathy, a commitment to understanding and healing the wounds that separate us.

Question: How often do you celebrate little victories? How often do you commend yourself for a job well done?

Chapter Seven

The Clown

From the moment I entered this world, it seemed like laughter was my birthright. I can almost picture myself emerging from my mòther's womb with a mischievous grin, ready to charm the world. Throughout my life, making people laugh has been as natural to me as breathing. Even in elementary school, I had my classmates and strangers alike in stitches with little effort. However, my knack for humor often landed me in trouble. As the class clown, I struggled to know when to rein it in, leading to frequent visits to the principal's office where the threat of suspension or a paddling loomed over me.

Despite the challenges, I possessed an innate ability to find humor in any situation. This improvisational skill, honed through years of quick wit and clever wordplay, became my trademark. It served me well while working in a state prison and jail where darkness permeated every corner. In those grim confines, where hope seemed like a distant memory, I found solitude and comfort in the power of laughter.

My duties as a prison employee often involved conducting security rounds and conversing with inmates. Each encounter was a delicate dance between maintaining authority and fostering human connection. The prison walls echoed stories of shattered dreams, lost dignity, and the heavy burden of regret.

Despite the weight of the environment, I refused to let despair consume me. Instead, I used humor as a lifeline, a light in the darkness. Through laughter, I forged bonds with inmates and colleagues alike, offering a brief respite from the harsh realities of prison life.

But behind the laughter lay a more profound truth—the trauma of working in such an environment takes its toll, leaving invisible scars to the naked eye. For the past seven years, I have dedicated myself to bridging the gap between law enforcement and the community, advocating for the recognition and treatment of trauma within the profession.

In the world of corrections, survival isn't just a matter of physical safety—it's about preserving one's humanity and mental health in an environment where darkness looms at every turn. As a corrections officer in the Florida Penal system, I quickly realized that my most valuable tools were not weapons but my ability to communicate and bring moments of light into the shadows.

Entering the academy, I was taken aback by the knowledge of an absence of firearms within the prison walls. Instead, officers relied on a radio, a set of keys, and the power of dialogue. It was a stark reminder that communication was not just a skill but a lifeline in this world. In a housing unit teeming with sixty or more inmates, many serving lengthy sentences and some with nothing to lose, the ability to navigate conversations with humor became paramount for both my survival and theirs.

I consciously tried to maintain professionalism while being firm and empathetic to those incarcerated. I never mock an inmate or their situation; instead, I focused on shared experiences outside prison walls. We talked about the shows we watched and the memories that felt like distant dreams in their reality of prison life. It was a delicate dance, a balancing act between authority and empathy, but I mastered with finesse, constantly reminded of their ability to manipulate.

But the toll of such an environment doesn't end when the shift does. Transitioning to work as a road patrol deputy brought its own set of challenges, as I encountered tragedy after tragedy on the streets. Humor became my therapist. Whether it was sharing a laugh with my zone partners to ease the weight of the day or using humor to navigate through gruesome scenes, laughter became my armor against the pain that threatened to consume me.

Law enforcement is an unpredictable profession. Chaos does not have a schedule nor a time. Does it care what kind of day you are having? It is up to us to find tools that lead us through the darkness. As a school resource deputy, I discovered that laughter provided a dopamine hit to help me through the day.

During these moments, I truly felt the impact of humor on myself and those around me. Growing up in an era of "Yo Momma" jokes, I understood the power of humor to transcend generational divides. While I never engaged in the banter myself, I stood by as a guardian, ensuring that playful exchanges didn't escalate into something darker.

But it wasn't just about preventing conflict—it was about bringing joy to the lives of the students I encountered. I vividly remember the weight that seemed to burden some of them as they trudged through the hallways, the weight of the world evident in their weary expressions. A well-timed joke or a playful quip could lift their spirits in those moments, if only for a fleeting moment. It was a gift I cherished, the ability to bring a smile to someone's face during their struggles.

Reflecting on my time working in schools, I recall the laughter that permeated the air, contrasting with the often-somber atmosphere. Sometimes, I would smile because I saw myself in the class clowns who used humor as a shield against the harsh realities of life. I witnessed the transformation of students who, despite their anger and frustration, found momentary relief in laughter.

In my law enforcement journey, the laughter that echoed through the school halls reminded me of the complexity of my role. It wasn't just about apprehending criminals or thwarting potential threats—it was about being supportive of and compassionate for the students, including those I had previously arrested.

As I navigated the challenges of protecting children in a world fraught with dangers, I realized that my responsibility extended far beyond the confines of campus security. It was about alleviating their burdens, whether from the demands of academia or the struggles they faced at home. It was about offering hope in the face of adversity, reminding them that each day was a fresh opportunity to start anew.

Laughter became my tool for connection and healing, a bridge that transcended the barriers of mistrust and resentment. It allowed me to set aside any personal grievances and extend a hand of empathy, offering solace to those in need. Whether it was a comforting touch, a listening ear, or simply a tissue to wipe away tears, laughter became a catalyst for genuine human connection.

But behind the laughter lay a deeper truth—a truth that spoke to the profound impact of trauma on both officers and the communities they served. It was a truth that I, as a certified emotional intelligence trainer, understood all too well. The scars of trauma run deep, manifesting not only in outward behaviors but also in the silent struggles that weigh heavy on the soul.

That's My DJ

1999 was a year of change for me. Remember that I had recently returned to work at the jail. An unexpected opportunity arose that would serve to carry me forward for decades. It was a time marked by the finalization of my second divorce, a period fraught with emotional turmoil and financial strain. During this time, my friend and co-worker, Mike, approached me with a proposition that seemed to offer some hope for my financial obligations. He proposed starting a Karaoke and DJ business, which promised financial stability and a creative outlet.

With Mike's offer to provide the initial capital for equipment, software, and music, we embarked on this new venture together, driven by a shared passion for music and entertainment. Mike's technical expertise complemented my natural flair for performance, making us a dynamic duo from the outset.

As we delved into the world of DJ gigs, we encountered the grueling reality of the business—a demanding schedule that took a toll on our 'spare time.'. We worked tirelessly, from late-night gigs at local bars to early morning shifts at our day jobs. It was a relentless cycle of hustle and exhaustion, a testament to our determination to make ends meet.

Despite the challenges, our efforts paid off, and for two glorious years, we basked in the success of our venture. We entertained crowds, filled dance floors, and left a lasting impression wherever we went. It was a brief break from the trials of life, a reminder that moments of joy were still within grasp.

As swiftly as our success had come, it was accompanied by its trials and tribulations. The toll of the business on our bodies and personal lives became increasingly apparent, and eventually, we decided to take a break and recover. I knew it was the right thing to do, but I had become accustomed to the money and the distraction that being a DJ afforded. I was still in the aftermath of divorce and financial strain. Mike, my friend and business partner, approached me with the opportunity to take sole ownership of our karaoke and DJ business. Perhaps he sensed the weight of my financial burdens and saw in me the resilience to carry the torch forward.

Though I lacked experience in running a business or marketing, I held steadfast to the belief in the power of 'word of mouth.' It became my guiding principle as I set out to expand our clientele, securing gigs at birthday and anniversary parties. Despite charging less than other DJs, I viewed it as a side hustle to supplement my career—a safety net amidst the uncertainty.

As the demand for our services grew, I found myself thrust into unfamiliar territory—DJing weddings, including ceremonies—an endeavor for which I was wholly unprepared. Yet, fueled by determination and a willingness to learn, I turned to resources like YouTube to glean the basics, improvising the rest as I went along.

Despite my initial apprehension, I soon found my stride, earning praise for my ability to entertain and keen ear for music. Whether performing behind a modest trailer in remote locales or commanding the stage at upscale venues, I adapted seamlessly to each setting, drawing upon my innate ability to read a crowd and create an unforgettable experience.

Yet, beneath the surface of success lay a more profound truth rooted in the challenges I grappled with as a business owner. "Imposter Syndrome," the inner self-doubt, gnawed at me, leaving a feeling of insecurity and uncertainness of my worth. It was a painful reminder of my journey, a journey marked by both triumphs and tribulations.

As the years have passed, my time as a DJ continues to reverberate through the present. People often approached me, reminiscing about the joy I brought to their special occasions many years ago. I receive their compliments with gratitude and humility, recognizing my unique gift to ease discomfort and bring laughter to even the most challenging moments.

It's a testament to the power of human connection that I've encountered individuals I've arrested at these celebratory events. Yet, our interactions have been smooth and without incident. It speaks volumes about the importance of treating everyone with dignity and respect, regardless of their circumstances.

Though these events were celebratory, a shadow lurked—a darkness within that threatened to overshadow the joyous atmosphere. As I strived to make my clients' special days memorable, I was often confronted with my inner demons, battling against the sadness and trauma that lingered just beneath the surface.

It was a delicate balancing act, one that required me to push down the darkness while maintaining a façade of celebration. Yet, through it all, I was reminded of the resilience that lies within each of us—the ability to rise above our pain and channel our experiences into moments of connection and joy.

Reflecting on my journey as a DJ, I am struck by the complexity of the human experience—the interplay of joy and sorrow, laughter and pain. It's a journey marked by moments of triumph and struggle, each contributing to the tapestry of my life.

How do you connect with those you serve?

Tears of a Clown

Growing up in the 70s, the soulful melodies of Motown provided a soundtrack to my childhood. I can still vividly recall the sound of Diana Ross and the Supremes filling the airwaves, their voices carrying tales of love and heartache. The Temptations and the Four Tops echoed through our home, their music intertwining with the rhythms of everyday life.

I loved the infectious beats and soulful harmonies, especially Smokey Robinson, who captivated my young heart. I remember being transfixed by his velvety voice, so rich with emotion and depth. As a child, I couldn't comprehend how such a powerful voice could belong to a man, a realization that only deepened my admiration as I grew older.

Listening to Smokey Robinson's music was more than just entertainment—it was a refuge, a sanctuary where I could lose myself in the stories woven within each song. The lyrics spoke of lost love and heartache, themes that resonated deeply with me, even at a young age.

In particular, the song "The Tracks of My Tears" struck a chord within me. Its lyrics mirrored the pain and struggles I encountered in my chosen career in law enforcement.

The lines,

"But don't let my glad expression,

Give you the wrong impression,

Really, I'm sad, Oh, I'm sadder than sad,"

His lyrics represented my emotions—the false sense of strength I presented to the world, masking the inner turmoil and sadness that often consumed me.

As the song continued, the lyrics spoke of masking one's pain with a veneer of carefreeness, a sentiment that resonated deeply with my experiences.

"Now if I appear to be carefree,

It's only to camouflage my sadness,

In order to shield my pride,

I try, to cover this hurt with a show of gladness,"

The words seemed to echo the internal struggle I faced daily as I navigated the complexities of my profession.

Through the music of Motown and artists like Smokey Robinson, I found peace and understanding in a world that had shown neither at times. Motown Music became a lifeline, a reminder that I was not alone in my struggles and that even in the darkest moments, there was beauty to be found.

I recall when someone half-jokingly questioned my demeanor, asking, "Why are you smiling? I thought cops were supposed to look mean and intimidating." It reminded me of the stereotypes that often surround law enforcement, yet I remained steadfast in my belief that empathy and approachability were vital to building trust within the community.

Adaptability became my greatest asset as I navigated the diverse situations I encountered on duty. Whether I was pursuing a fleeing felon or assisting an elderly lady searching for her misplaced keys, I approached each scenario with the appropriate level of intensity and compassion.

But beyond the uniform and badge, questions arose about my demeanor in everyday life. "Why are you smiling all the time?" some would inquire, while others wondered, "What are you so happy about?" On the surface, I exuded laughter and smiles, but internally, a different narrative unfolded—a narrative of inner turmoil and emotional pain.

For years, I wore the mask of the clown, laughing on the outside while grappling with my demons within. The laughter and smiles served as a facade, concealing the tears of a soul weighed down by the burdens of duty and trauma. My greatest fear was not the dangers lurking in the shadows—the meth addicts or the crack dealers—but rather the silent battles fought within the depths of my own psyche.

As I reflect on my journey, I am reminded of the complexity of the human experience—the dichotomy of strength and vulnerability, laughter and tears. It's a journey marked by moments of triumph and struggle, each contributing to the tapestry of my life.

In the relentless rhythm of my twelve-hour shifts, I remained vigilant, ever mindful of officer safety and situational awareness. But beneath the disguise of professionalism and caution lied the fear of the dam within me bursting open, unleashing a torrent of emotions I could no longer contain.

To prevent the dam from crumbling under the weight of my suppressed pain, I resorted to patchwork solutions—temporary fixes that offered fleeting relief but failed to address the root of my anguish. Alcohol became my chosen form of patchwork, a liquid painkiller that promised to numb the ache within.

After a long day on duty, I would return home, shedding the uniform and reaching for that first cold beer from the refrigerator. In those moments, I justified my actions, convincing myself I deserved this respite after the challenges I faced on the job. The safety of my home became my sanctuary, a haven where I could drown my sorrows without fear of judgment or consequence.

Initially, the alcohol served its purpose, soothing my frayed nerves and dulling the sharp edges of my pain. But as the hours wore on, the temporary relief gave way to a deeper darkness—a depressive state fueled by the toxic cocktail of alcohol and unresolved trauma.

In the depths of my despair, I found myself engulfed by a whirlwind of negative thoughts and memories, each layer of pain peeling back to reveal wounds I had long suppressed. Alcohol became the trigger that propelled me into the abyss, but the darkness that consumed me ran far deeper than the surface level.

As I grappled with the repercussions of my reliance on alcohol, I realized that true healing could not be achieved through patchwork solutions or temporary fixes. The dam within me demanded more than a Band-Aid—it required introspection, self-awareness, and a willingness to confront the demons that lurked within.

And so, my journey towards healing began—a journey marked by courage, vulnerability, and a commitment to addressing the trauma that had long plagued me. As a certified emotional intelligence trainer, I am driven by a profound sense of purpose—to help others in law enforcement understand the importance of addressing their own trauma and finding healthier coping mechanisms to navigate the challenges of their profession.

Question: Are you using patches in an attempt to fix what's going on in your life? Are you prepared for when those patches no longer hold?

Walk, Run, Walk Or Cry, In The End, It Doesn't Even Matter

At the age of thirty-nine, I found myself at a crossroads. Tired of carrying the physical and emotional weight that had accumulated over the years, I knew it was time for a change. Standing at 6'2" and weighing in at 250 pounds, the toll of poor eating habits and frequent bar visits had taken its toll. But it wasn't just about shedding pounds but about reclaiming my health and rediscovering a sense of purpose beyond work.

Aware of the looming specter of my father's heart attack at an early age, I knew I couldn't afford to wait any longer. So, I decided to go back to my roots of running. I missed the rhythmic beat of my feet hitting the pavement. Then, I stumbled upon a program called 'Run Walk Run'—a structured approach to running that emphasized intervals of walking and running, gradually increasing pace and distance over time.

As the weeks passed, I found myself becoming increasingly proficient in the program. Drawing upon the foundation of running instilled in me during high school, I felt a renewed sense of vitality coursing through my veins. But it wasn't just physical; running became my refuge, a sanctuary where I could escape the burdens of my job and the weight of my past.

I vividly remember crossing the finish line of my first 5k race—a modest achievement by some standards but a monumental victory for me. I pushed myself further with each race, setting new goals and surpassing my expectations. Before long, I was placing in my age division, fueling my determination to push the boundaries of what I thought possible.

But it was during a 5k race in Orlando, Florida, that fate once again paid me a visit in a most unexpected way. My wife and I were each awarded a free entry into the Daytona Beach Half-Marathon—a daunting challenge that neither of us had tackled. Yet rather than viewing it as an insurmountable obstacle, we embraced it as an opportunity to test our limits and conquer new heights together.

In the following five months, my wife and I embarked on a journey of preparation. We immersed ourselves in a sea of knowledge, devouring every piece of literature on training for a half-marathon we could find. From articles and books to instructional videos on YouTube, we absorbed every tidbit of information, determined to conquer this new challenge together.

Training became more than physical exertion—it became a shared experience that brought us closer as a couple. In our home routine, we delved into rigorous hours of preparation. Running up and down the stairs became a staple of our training regimen, as did navigating the 50-yard descent to the nearby lake. This picturesque backdrop served as both a sanctuary and a training ground.

Incorporating walking sessions into our daily routine, we gradually increased our mileage, pushing our bodies to new limits. As the miles accumulated, so too did the stresses of daily life. Running became a cathartic release, a means of shedding not just pounds but the burdens of our past.

Sharing our journey on social media, we encountered both praise and skepticism from friends and acquaintances alike. "Why would you guys go and run 9 and 10 miles at five in the morning?" they questioned, unable to comprehend the allure of our pre-dawn excursions. But for us, the answer was simple—it was about more than just physical fitness; it was about reclaiming control of our lives, one stride at a time.

As our bodies transformed, so too did our relationship. Only a year into our marriage, we laid the foundation for a future built on shared goals and mutual support. Despite our differing physical attributes—my towering stature juxtaposed against my wife's diminutive frame—we found unity in our pursuit of a common goal.

Each race brought us closer together as we discovered the true power of resilience and determination. Crossing the finish line, whether together or apart, was not just a triumph of physical endurance, but a testament to the strength of our bond—a bond forged through sweat, tears, and unwavering commitment.

Continuing my relentless pursuit of self-improvement, I incorporated weight training into my daily routine, determined to become a stronger, more resilient runner. I honed my skills and pushed my body to new limits; the accolades began to roll in, with finisher medals stacking up and victories in my age group category.

Though there were triumphs, there was also fear and anxiety as my wife and I prepared to tackle the Daytona Beach Half-Marathon. Despite having covered the distance in training, race day brought with it a palpable sense of anticipation and nerves.

As I stood amid the throng of runners, waiting for the starting pistol to sound, I found comfort in small talk and exchange of pleasantries, attempting to quell the butterflies fluttering in my stomach. When that starting gun finally went off, time seemed to slow to a crawl as I settled into my stride.

Equipped with my newly acquired Garmin watch, I monitored my pace, ensuring I stayed within the confines of a 9 minutes and 30 seconds per mile. With each step, I felt a sense of liberation wash over me, as if I were conquering the limits of my body.

By mile six, I found myself floating on air, buoyed by the euphoria of the runner's high—a sensation I had only heard about but never truly experienced until that moment. Passing by fellow runners grappling with cramps and fatigue, I felt an overwhelming sense of vitality coursing through my veins.

I ascended the bridge that loomed before me, the Daytona Beach Speedway came into view, signaling the imminent end of my two-hour journey. With the finish line in sight, I summoned the last reserves of my strength, propelled forward by a sense of purpose and determination that eclipsed any physical pain or fatigue I was experiencing.

Entering the speedway again was like stepping into the arena of my dreams, with the finish line beckoning me forward like a beacon of triumph. With just a quarter of a lap to go, I decided to tap into the depths of my inner strength and unleash a sprint unlike any other. I surged past fellow runners, some attempting to keep pace while others cheered me on. I felt an exhilarating rush of adrenaline coursing through my veins.

When I crossed the finish line in two hours and nine minutes, I was overcome with a sense of pride and accomplishment that words could scarcely capture. The weight of the finisher's medal around my neck served as a tangible reminder of the journey I had undertaken—a journey marked by perseverance, determination, and unwavering resolve.

But between the euphoria of my achievement, my heart swelled with pride as I watched my wife cross the finish line, her face radiant with joy and triumph. Standing by her side, I felt an overwhelming sense of gratitude for her support and companionship that had carried us through every step of our journey.

Buoyed by our success, my wife and I embarked on a new challenge—training for a marathon. We embraced a vegetarian lifestyle, finding nourishment and sustenance in the bountiful offerings of clean, natural plants and beans.

The months that followed were a demonstration of our dedication and resilience as we pushed each other to new heights, both physically and emotionally. With each sunrise, we would lace up our running shoes and hit the pavement, embarking on a journey of self-discovery and transformation.

As the 2010 Yuengling Marathon in Virginia Beach drew near, I found dealing with a potent mix of excitement and dread. Despite my rigorous training regimen, the prospect of tackling 26.2 miles loomed large on the horizon, a daunting challenge that tested the limits of my endurance and resolve.

Yet, aside from the uncertainty and anticipation, there remained hope—a belief that with determination and a 'can-do' spirit, anything was possible. I also took the approach that no matter the outcome, the journey itself had already been a victory.

The day of the Yuengling Marathon arrived with a mix of anticipation and nerves coursing through my veins. I stood at the starting line, surrounded by fellow runners, and couldn't help but feel a sense of anxiousness mingled with excitement. I had trained diligently for this moment, logging countless miles and adhering to a strict regimen in preparation for the grueling race ahead.

As the miles ticked by and the rhythm of my stride carried me forward, I felt a creeping sense of unease settle in the pit of my stomach. Around mile 14, a nagging sensation of discomfort began to tug, but I pushed through, attributing it to pre-race jitters. With each passing mile, the struggle intensified, my pace faltering as the physical demand of the marathon took its toll on my body.

By mile 17, I found myself face to face with the infamous "wall"—that dreaded barrier that separates the determined from the defeated. My legs felt like lead, my muscles protesting with every step as I battled to keep moving forward. It was a moment of reckoning, a test of endurance and mental fortitude unlike any I had faced before.

Summoning every ounce of strength within me, I soldiered on, fueled by sheer determination and the support of my fellow runners. The journey to the finish line was a grueling odyssey fraught with pain and self-doubt, but I refused to succumb to defeat.

When I crossed the finish line in 5 hours and 9 minutes, I was met with a whirlwind of emotions—disappointment in my finishing time mingled with pride and exhaustion tinged with triumph. The weight of the finisher's medal around my neck served as a tangible reminder of the arduous journey I had undertaken—less than one percent of the world population has completed a marathon.

Despite falling short of my expectations, my wife's words of encouragement comforted me in my disappointment. Her belief in my abilities helped soften my feelings of defeat and reminded me that there is still cause for celebration and gratitude, even in moments of perceived failure.

Months would pass, and I found myself training for another marathon. I had several months to prepare for my next endeavor. This time, I was determined to do everything right. I would follow a strict diet, remain hydrated, and hire a coach if necessary. Deep down, I felt I had left too much on the road and knew I could do better. The training could not have been going better. I added weight training to my regimen, and my weekly training times improved.

It was a Thursday morning. I had peaked in my exercises and was on schedule with my training. I was smiling as I completed a middle-distance training run. As I sprinted towards the finish line of my 9-mile run, the familiar sight of my front door beckoned to me from the end of our cul-de-sac. With each stride, I felt a surge of adrenaline coursing through my veins, propelling me forward with unwavering determination. But as I neared the end of my sprint, disaster struck—a sudden, searing pain shot through my groin, bringing me to an abrupt halt.

In that moment, the confidence and euphoria I had cultivated since my last marathon evaporated, replaced by a wave of agony and uncertainty. I grasped at my leg, hoping against hope that it was nothing more than a pulled muscle, but deep down, I knew it was something far worse.

As I hobbled back towards my house, each step sent waves of pain radiating through my body, a stark reminder of my vulnerability and mortality. It was a humbling experience, a harsh reminder that even the strongest among us are not immune to injury and setbacks.

Upon reaching my front door, I collapsed onto the ground, clutching at my throbbing leg as the reality of my situation sank in. I had pushed myself too hard, too fast, and now I was paying the price for my recklessness.

In the days and weeks that followed, I dealt with the physical and emotional toll of my injury, dealing with feelings of frustration, anger, and despair. The road to recovery was long and arduous, marked by setbacks and moments of doubt, but through it all, I refused to give up hope.

With the support of my family and loved ones, I embarked on a journey of healing and self-discovery, determined to emerge more robust and more resilient than ever before. Although the road ahead would be challenging and full of obstacles, I faced each day with courage and conviction, knowing that with perseverance and determination, I would overcome whatever obstacles lay in my path.

In the end, my injury served as a powerful reminder of the fragility of life and the importance of self-care and mindfulness. It was a wake-up call, a clear reminder that even the most dedicated and driven among us must listen to our bodies and prioritize our health and well-being.

I refused to let this setback define me. Running had become a valuable tool to keep the demons at bay.

Question: Have you picked up a hobby that helps on your days off to focus on something positive?

Chapter Eight

Into The Darkness

As I sat in the waiting room of the orthopedic surgeon's office, that familiar sense of apprehension returned. Despite my attempts to remain calm and composed, the fear of what lay ahead occupied my every thought.

The orthopedic surgeon entered the room, his demeanor serious and focused. He listened intently as I recounted the events that had led me to his office, the lingering pain that refused to subside despite weeks of rest and physical therapy.

After a thorough examination, the surgeon delivered the news I had been dreading—my injury was far more severe than a simple groin strain. The X-rays showed what was not only a tear but what appeared to be arthritis, the surgeon ordered an MRI to be done as soon as possible.

Entering the Orthopedic office felt like stepping into a world of uncertainty and apprehension. The air was heavy with the weight of my fears, each breath a struggle against the suffocating sense of dread that gripped my chest.

As I sat in the waiting room, the minutes stretched into eternity, each tick of the clock a painful reminder of the uncertainty ahead. When I was finally called back to the examination room, my heart hammered in my chest, the rhythm irregular and discordant, mirroring the chaos of my thoughts.

The doctor entered the room, his expression grim and devoid of empathy. Without a preamble, he held up the X-rays, his words cutting through the silence like a knife. "You are going to need your right hip replaced," he declared, his tone indifferent. "Your hip is eaten up with arthritis."

I felt like the ground had dropped from beneath me, leaving me suspended in a void of disbelief and denial. How could this be happening? I had always prided myself on my physical strength and resilience, and yet here I was, facing the prospect of a life-altering surgery.

I felt a wave of panic wash over me as the reality of my situation sank in. Surgery was not something I had ever anticipated, especially not for a running injury. How could there be arthritis? I'm only 40! The thought of being sidelined for weeks, possibly even months, filled me with a profound sense of despair.

In a daze, I stumbled out of the office, the weight of the doctor's words bearing down on me like a leaden weight. Anger bubbled up inside me, hot and searing, a molten rage threatening to consume me from within.

I sought out second opinions and third opinions, clinging to the hope that someone, somewhere, would offer a glimmer of hope in the darkness that threatened to engulf me. But with each consultation, the reality of my situation became increasingly clear—there was no escaping the certainty of my diagnosis.

As I made my way home, anger gave way to despair, and tears flowed freely as I grappled with the unfairness of it all. "Why me?" I cried out to the heavens, my voice cracking with the weight of my anguish. What have I done to deserve this?"

But even in my despair, some hope remained—a stubborn ember that refused to be extinguished. I made an appointment with a renowned orthopedic center, determined to explore every option, no matter how daunting or uncertain.

The surgeon who greeted me radiated warmth and compassion, his demeanor a stark contrast to the cold indifference of the doctor who had delivered my diagnosis. He took the time to explain my condition in detail, offering reassurance and hope in equal measure.

As the day of surgery approached, the weight of anticipation hung heavy in the air, each passing moment laden with a sense of foreboding. Despite my outward bravado on social media, I couldn't shake the gnawing tendrils of sadness that coiled around my soul, threatening to drag me into the abyss of despair.

On the morning of my first-ever surgery, I found myself standing on the precipice of uncertainty, my heart heavy with the weight of unspoken fears. In quiet desperation, I turned to a higher power, praying for guidance and strength. With a heavy heart, I sought forgiveness for the bitterness and anger that had consumed me in the darkest hours of my despair, promising to emerge from this trial a better, more compassionate version of myself.

As I lay on the gurney, preparing to face the unknown, my youngest brother, Ross, newly ordained into the ministry, offered a silent prayer to comfort me. His presence with my wife gave me hope that everything would be alright.

The surgery was filled with unexpected challenges, the surgeon's skillful hands navigating the tangled web of muscles. Due to my runner's muscles, which took much longer to cut through, the surgery took longer than expected. Hours stretched into what seemed like an eternity as my wife waited anxiously for news; with each passing moment, she became increasingly concerned.

When the surgeon finally emerged from the operating room, he appeared to have just left the frontline of a battle. Sweat marks pocked his scrubs, and his hair resembled the infamous Einstein. Despite the successful outcome of the surgery, the road to recovery would be painful. I couldn't help thinking that this was the price I was paying for attempting to outrun my demons.

The first day of recovery was a blur of agony and despair. The onslaught of muscle spasms and the demands of the physical therapy machine attached to my leg threatened to tear me apart. As the hours stretched into eternity, I found myself grappling with the darkest depths of physical pain I had ever known.

Amid my suffering, my wife became my champion, advocating tirelessly on my behalf in the face of a pretty indifferent caregiver and her subsequent neglect during my hospital stay. My wife became my lifeline, guiding me through the darkest hours of my recovery with steadfast love and compassion.

After two grueling days in the hospital, I was finally released to start rehabilitation and to relearn how to walk—armed with little more than a walker and my anger. I started my journey into the unfamiliar terrain of post-surgical recovery as the darkness threatened to engulf me, each step forward a painful reminder of the sacrifices I needed to make in pursuit of a life free from pain and suffering.

As the car rolled along the familiar streets toward home, a heavy silence settled between us, thick with unspoken fears and uncertainties. I struggled to find the words to articulate the storm raging within me, my mind a swirling vortex of confusion and disbelief. Lost in my thoughts, I struggled with the harsh reality of my situation, the pain of recent events still fresh and raw. I was no longer Fred, the runner.

My wife tended to my every need with tenderness and understanding. Though spoken with conviction, her words of encouragement felt like feeble whispers against the deafening roar of doubt that remained high pitch day and night.

During my rehabilitation journey, I sought support in the shared experiences of others who had walked this path before me. Scouring social media for glimpses of hope and inspiration, I clung to the stories of those who had emerged from the ordeal of their struggles, hoping their triumphs would provide me with much-needed hope.

I took up walking at a familiar and comforting place: the local high school running track. With each tentative step around the track, my walker became a physical crutch and a metaphorical lifeline, guiding me to recovery. Rehabilitation is one of the most painful experiences of my life. It was not just the physical pain; it was the absence of my soul which was unbearable.

I smiled at my social media posts; some were sincere, while others were forced. What I dreaded most about the days of rehabilitation was days eventually turned into nights. I spent my nights in a recliner, along with my thoughts. The nights were when my demons waged war with my ego; the demons always won.

As the days stretched into weeks and the weeks into months, the relentless march of time became a cruel reminder of the slow, agonizing pace of my recovery. I lived in frustration and despair at the edge of my sanity.

I found moments to cherish through it all. As my wife captured snapshots of my progress, I played the role of the dutiful patient, smiling through the pain and pretending that everything was alright, if only for a moment. Some of the moments were real.

I declared war on the nights, using a bottle of bourbon and whisky as my weapon. I found myself wielding the sword of Crown Royal, seeking refuge and revenge simultaneously. With each sip, the darkness would go away for a moment—at least, that's the story I told myself. In the throes of my addiction, I had become a slave to the bottle, a prisoner of my own making. Yet, in my distorted reality, I clung to the false promise that each empty bottle held the key to my salvation.

Despite my wife's genuine praise and encouragement, her words fell upon deaf ears. I lived in self-doubt and anger. My anger and depression got worse even though physically I was getting stronger. The only thing I could focus on was what I had lost. I found myself lashing out at the one person who stood unwaveringly by my side, my anchor, my wife. Yet, even in moments of rage and despair, her arms remained open to me, always welcoming.

Years later, when reflecting on my journey through the crucible of hip replacement surgery, I would often find myself grappling with the question: "What was the most challenging aspect of the entire ordeal?" For me, the answer lay not in the physical pain or the arduous path of rehabilitation but in the shattering realization that my identity as a law enforcement officer was forever altered.

The mantra "To Protect and Serve" had been ingrained in my psyche for over 15 years, a guiding principle that defined my purpose and identity. Yet, the words of my doctor, delivered with the blunt force of a freight train, shattered my sense of self. I was told that I would never be able to perform the duties of a law enforcement officer again fully. It was a devastating blow to my spirit, a seismic shift that left me reeling.

However, that wreckage was not the worst of it; a far more profound and heart-wrenching question lingered: "Would I be able to protect my wife if necessary?" The answer echoed through my soul with relentless clarity - a resounding 'No.' How could I, a crippled shadow of my former self, ever hope to shield her from harm?

As I continued my rehabilitation journey, each step forward felt like a Herculean effort. I knew deep in my heart that I would never be the same person again, but could I somehow become a better person? Four weeks into my journey, I had transitioned to walking without the aid of a walker, relying only on a cane for support when venturing outside.

Despite my incremental progress, I still perceived myself as insufficient. How do I bounce back from this darkness? How do I find purpose again? What If I can't return to my identity as a deputy sheriff? Who would I become? Would my wife still want me? Those questions and so many others assaulted me daily.

One day, my wife surprised me with a gift that aided my physical and emotional recovery - a dog.

A friend of hers recounted the tale of a malnourished dog he had encountered in a wooded area, a creature needing love and care. It took hours of patient coaxing and gentle gestures before this dog finally allowed him to approach with a treat, a gesture of trust that would forever impact our lives. This friend insisted that he would indeed become divorced if he took this dog home, for he already found four other dogs in his house. One call to my wife, and he was on his way to us.

He arrived on our doorstep like he knew he belonged there. A tremendous hulking form of a canine at approximately 100 pounds of husky-labrador mix. He walked over to us and performed the infamous 'labrador-lean.' From that distinct moment, I felt another Universal Message was being delivered in the shape of a creature who had known pain and hardship. He was bony and malnourished, yet he smiled. Homeless, yet hopeful.

As the days turned into weeks and months, our bond with the dog we named 'Sammy' increased. Sammy was a striking mix of yellow lab and husky; he soon became integral to our family. His mismatched eyes, blue and brown, seemed to reflect the complexity of emotions I grappled with daily. Despite his size, Sammy's gentle and loving demeanor endeared him to everyone he met. Whenever we mentioned going outside, his enthusiastic barks were a source of delight and laughter for us.

With each wag of his tail and gentle nuzzle, he reminds us of the importance of staying present. He didn't whine about what happened to him. He didn't complain that he was abandoned or abused. He was always the light to be found in the embrace of those who love us unconditionally.

In the presence of our canine companion, I found solace and strength, a silent companion who walked beside me through the darkest depths of my despair. He became my constant companion, a source of comfort and inspiration as I navigated the turbulent waters of my recovery. Sammy became my steadfast companion, accompanying me on daily walks and providing the motivation I needed to meet my doctor's prescribed step count. With each step I took alongside Sammie, I felt a sense of progress and accomplishment, a tangible reminder that I was slowly regaining control of my life.

Returning to work after months of rehabilitation was a bittersweet experience. The warm welcome and heartfelt congratulations from colleagues gave me a sense of validation and belonging. Yet, amidst the laughter and camaraderie of the workplace, there lingered a palpable sense of unease and apprehension.

The afternoons were the toughest when the bustle of the school day had faded away. Alone with my thoughts, I found myself grappling with a tidal wave of self-doubt and insecurity. The demons of doubt and unworthiness whispered incessantly in my ear, their voices growing louder and more insistent as the shadows lengthened.

In the solitude of the evening, as my wife retired to bed, I once again found alcohol as a means of numbing the pain that gnawed at my soul. It was not the physical pain of my recovery that tormented me but the deep-seated anguish of losing my sense of identity and purpose. The ache of not being the Fred Jones who had once conquered half marathons with ease but a mere shadow of his former self plagued me daily.

In the daily grind of struggles and triumphs of law enforcement, a narrative often goes untold. It's the story of inner battles fought in silence, the struggle to maintain integrity while in the middle of chaos, and the journey of healing that transcends physical recovery. This is my story, a story that echoes the silent cries of countless officers and their families who navigate trauma and emotional turmoil in silence. Men and women wearing badges are not often encouraged to discuss their fears. They are trained to bear harsh realities and watch endless stories of human suffering.

As I sat there, bourbon in hand, the weight of my thoughts pressed heavily upon me while I searched for hope. The words from the book of Job reverberated in my mind, a haunting reminder of the relentless onslaught of challenges that seemed to test the essence of my being. Despite the unwavering support of my loving wife and the comforting presence of my loyal dog, Sammie, the darkness would not go away. I remember the words of Job's wife when she tried to convince him that God had abandoned him and he should curse God and die.

It wasn't for lack of trying or the absence of external signs of progress. Back at work, surrounded by co-workers who understood the intricacies of the profession, I appeared to be moving forward in my recovery. My surgeon's reassurances of a swift physical recovery stayed on my mind, but the reality was far from it. While my body may have regained its strength, my mind lagged. Instead of being present, I focused on my limitations.

Every day, like clockwork, I completed my walks; I couldn't help but feel a pang of envy as runners whizzed past me with determination etched on their faces. The familiar ache of longing stirred within me, a longing to experience the rush of adrenaline, the pounding of feet against pavement, and the sheer exhilaration of pushing my body to its limits. But it was a reality I had to face – a reality that I would never again feel the wind against my face as I sprinted towards the finish line.

Well-meaning friends suggested swimming as an alternative, a gesture of kindness veiled in concern. Yet, as the days stretched into weeks, my depression deepened, overshadowing any semblance of hope.

It was a Thursday in 2012, a day etched into my memory like a jagged scar. The rain, relentless and unforgiving, mirrored the storm within me. As I sat in the dimly lit living room, I felt as though the sky had opened up and was crying along with me. I remember the weight of my world pressing down on me, suffocating me like a heavy blanket. It felt as though the walls of my home were closing in on me. In that moment, I made a decision born out of desperation and despair. I no longer wanted to live; it was that simple. The person I was had died with my diagnosis. I was now a cripple in my mind's eye.

With trembling hands, I reached for the bottle of bourbon in the corner of the room. Its amber contents beckoned to me, promising solace in oblivion. I poured myself a glass, the liquid burning down my throat, a bitter reminder of my shattered dreams and unfulfilled promises.

As I sat there, drowning in self-pity and regret, I felt a sudden urge to leave behind a final farewell. With shaking hands, I retrieved my pen and paper, the words flowing from me like a river of anguish. Each stroke of the pen was a cathartic release, a testament to the agony that consumed me.

"Dearest Dana," I began, my voice trembling with emotion. "I'm sorry. I'm sorry for the man I've become, for the burdens I've placed upon your shoulders. I'm sorry for the pain I've caused and the promises I've broken. I no longer have the strength to carry on, to face the demons that haunt me."

Tears blurred my vision as I poured my heart onto that page; the ink smudged with the weight of my sorrow. As I reached the end of my letter, a sense of finality washed over me like a tidal wave. I was prepared to die.

But a familiar presence stirred beside me just as I prepared to end my torment. Sammy, my loyal companion, gazed up at me with concern. I could see in his expression he knew something was wrong. With a gentle nudge, he pushed me back into my chair, his loyalty a reminder that I was not alone.

I tried to rise again, but Sammy pressed once again, pushing me down in my chair and staring up at me. At that moment, as the rain continued to fall outside, I realized that we don't only live for ourselves; we can and should live for our loved ones until we're strong enough to resume living for ourselves.

The sound of the door opening shattered the eerie stillness that had settled over our home. The rain, which had pounded against the windows, had finally quieted, leaving behind a world drenched in silence. And there she was, my wife Dana; her presence was welcome. As our eyes met, a wave of emotion surged through me, threatening to engulf me in its tumultuous embrace. It was as if a dam inside me had burst, releasing a flood of tears that had been held back for far too long.

Dana approached me cautiously, her gaze filled with concern and compassion. As she wrapped her arms around me, things felt different this time; somehow, I knew it would be different. It's going to be okay," her voice filled with love. At that moment, I knew that she was right. But I also knew that I couldn't continue to suffer in silence and needed to reach out for help.

Through tear-filled eyes, I met Dana's gaze, my voice trembling as I voiced the words weighing heavily on my heart. "I need to talk to someone," I confessed, the admission a painful acknowledgment of what many of us never acknowledge.

Dana held me tighter, her embrace a lifeline in the storm. "Yes," she whispered, her voice filled with unwavering determination. "I will help love you through this."

We stood there, locked in each other's arms, I felt hope, real hope ignite within me, a small but resilient moment. With Dana (and Sammy) by my side and professional help, I knew that I could face whatever demons lurked in the shadows and that together, we could navigate my trauma and emerge stronger on the other side.

Question:

Have you ever reached a breaking point in your career or in your life? How did you handle it?

John Coffey

Opening up to another person, baring your soul in its rawest form, is akin to exposing a wound to the harsh light of day. It's a vulnerability that cuts deep, leaving you exposed and defenseless against the judgment of others. As I contemplated seeking help from a therapist, a barrage of doubts flooded my mind. How could this stranger possibly understand the depth of my pain? How could she judge me, having never walked in my shoes?

The thought of confronting the demons that lurked within me was daunting, akin to having teeth pulled without the numbing embrace of Novocain. But I knew that I couldn't continue to carry the weight of my trauma alone. So, with reluctance and a heavy heart, I took the first tentative steps towards healing.

In therapy, I embarked on a journey of self-discovery, delving deep into the recesses of my soul to confront the ghosts of my past. One of the most profound revelations came when I learned to forgive my thirteen-year-old self for his inability to save my fifteen-year-old brother from committing suicide. I had carried that guilt for decades, and it was negatively impacting my life. It was a lesson in self-compassion, a recognition that I couldn't be held responsible for the actions of others.

But forgiveness didn't come easy. It required me to confront the wreckage of failed relationships and the scars left by traumatic events that had haunted me for years. Through therapy, I learned to peel back the layers of pain and shame, exposing the raw wounds that festered beneath the surface.

As I unraveled my past, I found peace in the realization that it was okay to love myself—flaws and all. This revelation transformed the way I viewed myself and the world around me.

But perhaps the most transformative aspect of therapy was its ability to help me process the traumas I had witnessed during my time as a deputy. The memories of suicides and homicides, of shattered lives and grieving loved ones, had long haunted my dreams. But through the healing power of therapy, I was able to confront these demons head-on, pulling back the scabs that had long covered the wounds of my soul.

As I sat in front of the television, mindlessly flipping through channels, I stumbled upon one of my favorite movies, 'The Green Mile.' Little did I know that watching the scene where John Coffey, a character from Stephen King's novel, absorbed the sickness from the warden's wife was as if a bolt of lightning struck me. In that moment, I saw myself reflected in Coffey—a vessel for others' pain, a beacon of light in the darkness.

But unlike Coffey's fictional abilities, I couldn't simply absorb others' suffering and release it into the atmosphere. No, the burden of their pain weighed heavy on my soul, chipping away at my spirit with each passing day. It was a realization that shook me to my core – the more I gave of myself, the more I sacrificed, the less I had left to give.

For too long, I had lived under the illusion that my purpose was to bring happiness to others, to be the light in their darkest hour. But in doing so, I had neglected my well-being, burying my pain beneath a facade of selflessness.

Therapy was my lifeline, the key that unlocked the shackles binding me to my past traumas and insecurities. Through the power of introspection, I confronted the harsh truths I had long suppressed – the belief that I didn't deserve peace, love, or happiness and that my sole purpose was to serve others at the expense of my happiness.

But therapy was more than just a means of self-discovery—it was a journey of self-compassion, a process of learning to be kind to myself in ways I had never thought possible. It reminded me that I deserved to experience joy and fulfillment and that my well-being was just as important as the happiness of those around me.

So, armed with the lessons learned in therapy, I began a journey of self-care, learning to strike a balance between serving others and taking care of myself. It was a journey filled with ups and downs, triumphs and setbacks, but through it all, I emerged stronger, more resilient, and more compassionate toward myself and others.

Today, I stand before you not as a victim of my past traumas but as a survivor—hopefully an example to others who may be struggling to navigate the murky waters of their pain. As I continue on my healing journey, I am committed to helping others in my profession do the same, confront their demons head-on, and emerge stronger on the other side. For in the darkness of our pain lies the seed of our redemption, a testament to the spirit of the human soul.

The Second Time Around

In 2015, I found myself facing round two on the surgery table, this time for the replacement of my left hip. Despite the procedure's familiarity, a lingering apprehension weighed heavy on my heart. But this time, I was prepared. With my wife beside me, I braced myself for the journey ahead.

In the months leading up to the surgery, I connected with support groups. Some were preparing to undergo similar procedures. I immersed myself in hip replacement Facebook groups, offering encouragement and sharing my experiences with those about to embark on a journey I knew all too well.

But perhaps the most transformative aspect of this experience was the emotional journey I embarked on in the days leading up to the surgery. I shed the layers of shame and fear that had weighed me down for so long, learning to forgive myself for everything that had gone wrong in my life – even those things that were not my fault.

When I forgave myself, I discovered a newfound sense of peace that permeated every fiber of my being. It was a feeling unlike anything I had ever experienced, a sense of tranquility, a warm embrace.

The surgery was a success, and in the days and weeks that followed, I gradually regained my strength and mobility. There were still moments of vulnerability when I felt I was back at square one. Amidst uncertainty and discomfort, I clung to a newfound perspective rooted in mindfulness and intentional living. Through practice and deliberate thinking, I learned to focus on the present moment and embrace each step of the journey with gratitude and acceptance.

While working through my second surgery, I stumbled upon a documentary that spoke of the transformative power of nature, acting as a sanctuary. The video explained how walking in nature could lower cortisol levels, improve cardiovascular health, enhance creativity and focus, and even boost the immune system. It introduced the concept of ecotherapy, a form of therapy rooted in nature known to alleviate mild to moderate depression.

I navigated the challenges of rehabilitation and recovery; I did so with a sense of purpose and resilience. My past traumas or limitations no longer defined me; I was empowered by the lessons I had learned and the growth I had experienced.

In 2016, my agency sent me to a human diversity class unlike any other I had attended before. This training was not just about ticking boxes or fulfilling requirements; it was a deep dive into Emotional Intelligence – a topic that would soon become a cornerstone of my personal and professional development.

I realized that emotional intelligence was precisely what I needed to navigate the complexities of my own emotions and those of others. This revelation sparked a journey of self-discovery and growth.

One of the first lessons I learned was the importance of self-awareness. I kept a journal, meticulously documenting my thoughts and emotions and dissecting how they influenced my behavior. Through this practice, I gained a deeper understanding of myself—my strengths, weaknesses, and everything else.

But self-awareness was just the beginning. I also learned the art of self-regulation—the ability to harness my emotions in a way that benefited me and those around me. I no longer allowed my emotions to dictate my actions; I learned to express them constructively and healthily.

Empathy, too, became a cornerstone of my emotional intelligence journey. I had always prided myself on my ability to empathize with others, but now I was hyper-aware of the subtle nuances of human emotion. I could now sense the underlying fear hidden beneath the bravado of juveniles challenging my authority, their anger a shield to protect their vulnerability.

Emotional Intelligence became my shield against the pitfalls of time travel – the temptation to dwell on the past or fret about the future. I learned to live in the present moment, embracing each day with gratitude for everything I had. I developed mindfulness to address my habits and how they served me…or not.

Of course, my journey was not without its challenges. The limitations imposed by my double hip replacement were a constant reminder of my physical fragility. But this time, instead of dwelling on what I could no longer do, I focused on the positive – the strides I had made in my emotional well-being and the impact I could have on others.

In 2017, a new opportunity was presented to me… a journey to the Administrative Officers Course at the University of Louisville, a pivotal chapter in my quest for self-discovery and professional growth. As I prepared for this new chapter, I found myself drawn to the physical challenge of the Kentucky Derby Half-Marathon, a symbolic reminder of the resilience of both my mind and body.

Despite being five years removed from my first hip replacement and only two years from my left, I was determined to push my limits and prove that I could achieve greatness despite my physical limitations. With each step of my training regimen, I confronted the pain and discomfort that had become all too familiar, transforming it into fuel for my journey.

Upon arriving in Louisville in February 2017, I was greeted with the opportunity to immerse myself in three months of intensive leadership training. This experience would push me to the limits of my physical and emotional endurance. Embracing the curriculum enthusiastically, I established a rigorous walk/run training schedule around my academic commitments.

Each morning, before the sun had even risen, I would rise at 5 a.m. and make my way to the gym, where I would spend an hour on the treadmill, pushing myself to new heights of physical exertion. After a long day of classes and workshops, I would take to the streets, embarking on a grueling road jog/walk spanning five to six miles, depending on the demands of my training schedule.

In my quest for solace, I turned to the vast expanse of self-help materials, devouring blogs and YouTube videos in search of a lifeline amidst the chaos. During this search, I stumbled upon a video that spoke of the transformative power of nature, a sanctuary of tranquility amidst the tumult of life.

Despite the inevitable pain and discomfort that accompanied each step, I focused on the beauty of the Louisville area, exploring its scenic parks and tranquil landscapes as I pressed my body to its limits once again. Amidst the chaos of my training regimen, I found moments of profound meaning and purpose.

One such moment came a month into the leadership school when I participated in a 10k memorial run honoring a fallen law enforcement officer. It was a solemn yet empowering experience, a reminder of the sacrifices made by those who serve and protect our communities. As I crossed the finish line, a sense of pride and accomplishment washed over me, mingling with the pain and exhaustion that pulsed through my body. It was a moment of triumph, a testament to what's possible with the power of determination.

Running for My Life

On April 29th, 2017, a significant moment awaited me - a day I had anticipated since stepping foot in Louisville, Kentucky. It was a day of reckoning, a day where I would confront the ghosts of my past and redefine the trajectory of my future.

As the date drew nearer, anticipation mingled with excitement; I looked forward to the challenge ahead. For so long, I believed I was running towards something when, in reality, I was attempting to flee from the shadows of my past – a past marred by mistakes and regrets.

But now, standing on the cusp of a new beginning, I found myself propelled forward by a newfound sense of purpose. No longer content to merely exist, I was determined to embrace life with a new resolve to move toward a future defined by peace and clarity.

And so, as the starting gun echoed through the air and the crowd's cheers reverberated in my ears, I set out on my journey with a heart full of hope and determination. With each step, I felt the weight of my past fall away, replaced by a sense of exhilaration and freedom, unlike anything I had ever known.

My strategy was simple – walk for two minutes and jog for one, a rhythm recommended by experts. As I navigated the course, I felt a swell of pride wash over me; it felt good to be out here again.

Once I stood on the other side of that finish line, I bathed in the glow of victory. I finished the race! I was no longer concerned with how long it took. I knew that this physical journey I just completed was the start of what would come. I was headed on a mission that would forever shape my life. In that moment, I had conquered the physical distance and the barriers of doubt and fear that had once held me captive.

So, armed with this newfound knowledge, I resolved to seek refuge in the embrace of nature, to escape the suffocating confines of my mind, and to immerse myself in the healing embrace of the great outdoors. It was a decision born out of desperation, a last-ditch effort to silence the voices of doubt and reclaim control over my narrative.

As I ventured into the wilderness, each step a declaration of defiance against the forces that sought to hold me back, I found myself enveloped in a sense of peace unlike anything I had ever known. The serenity of the natural world is soothing for the soul and backed by science. In this sanctuary, the voices faded into the background, replaced by the gentle whispers of the wind and the soothing rustle of leaves.

My wife drove me to the park on a fateful Wednesday morning, a simple act of love. Yet, as we approached the lush greenery, the voices attempted to get louder, taunting me with doubts and fears. They tried to remind me of the looming hospital bills, urging me to focus on practicalities rather than seeking solitude in nature.

Stepping out of the car, I was greeted by the serene beauty of the park – a sea of green stretching out before me, a stark contrast to the chaos within. The tension and anxiety attempting to rise slowly dissipated, replaced by a sense of calm as I moved forward in mother nature.

With each step, I felt the weight of my burdens lift, transported back to a simpler time – a time of innocence and joy. Memories flooded my mind, cheering me back to my childhood, to days spent running through fields and playing in the woods with my brother and friends. It was when time seemed to stand still, and my only concern was making it home before the streetlights came on. Nature has the power to return our primitive brains to this peace.

Delving deeper into ecotherapy, I uncovered a wealth of studies affirming the healing power of nature. Scientific research revealed that spending time in natural surroundings expedites healing and recovery and boasts remarkable health benefits such as reducing blood pressure and lowering cancer risk. However, these findings merely echoed what I had long sensed in the depths of my soul – that nature was the ultimate remedy for the cacophony of voices that plagued my mind.

As I ventured further into the embrace of Mother Nature, I found myself drifting further from the chaos of the workplace and the relentless self-doubt that had haunted me for so long. With each step, the volume of the 'work voices' diminished, overshadowed by the serenity of the natural world. It was as though I had hit the mute button on my troubles, enveloped in a cocoon of tranquility as I immersed myself in the abundance of greenery. The crisp, fresh air filled my lungs, the melodic chirping of birds provided a soothing soundtrack, and, at times, the profound silence of the wilderness spoke volumes to my soul.

At the time of this publication, it has now been over a decade since my first hip replacement, nature remains my steadfast companion in navigating the workplace and everyday life stresses. It is a sanctuary where I find solace, a sacred space where the burdens of the past and the anxieties of the future melt away, leaving only the present moment to be savored and cherished. As I continue to walk this path of healing and self-discovery, I am reminded of the profound wisdom inherent in the natural world – that amidst the chaos of life, a timeless tranquility is waiting to be embraced.

Staying Present

Time travel has always fascinated me, much like the classic films I enjoy, such as Back to the Future. The notion of rewriting history, undoing past mistakes, and preventing future regrets is tempting. We yearn to alter the course of our lives, to spare ourselves the pain and heartache that inevitably accompany missteps.

Yet, as I've realized, time travel is a mere fantasy, an unattainable dream that teases us with the promise of redemption. Instead, I've found myself unwittingly traversing the corridors of my mind, journeying back to the darkest recesses of my past. Through the lens of memory, I revisit my most significant failures and my deepest regrets, and I'm forced to confront the ghosts of my past.

In these moments of reflection, my mind becomes a time machine of sorts, transporting me back to the most traumatic moments of my life, particularly those entangled in the web of relationships. I am mired in self-doubt, questioning my worth and ability to bring happiness to myself and those who have placed their faith in me.

But through the darkness, there resides a beacon of light that pierces through the shadows of my despair. It is the knowledge that while I may be powerless to change the past, I possess the agency to shape my future. Through introspection and self-awareness, I can learn from my mistakes, grow from my experiences, and ultimately chart a new course.

I am often reminded of the importance of confronting our inner demons and acknowledging the pain and trauma that lurk beneath the surface. Only by walking through our vulnerabilities can we hope to transcend them, emerging more substantial and more resilient on the other side.

Whenever I dared to peer into the future, it often gave me a sense of foreboding. Each leap forward in time brought with it a cascade of fears and anxieties, a bunch of "what ifs" that threatened to overwhelm me. "What if I lost my job?" "What if she says no when I ask her to marry me?" Fueled by the fires of doubt, these questions could ignite fear, doubt, and stagnation. The journey of time travel, undertaken within the confines of my mind, proved to be a challenging endeavor.

I embarked on a journey of self-discovery, a quest to reclaim control over my destiny amidst this tumultuous landscape of past regrets and future fears. Learning to anchor myself firmly in the present moment became my guiding principle. Yet, this transition was far from easy as I grappled with the weight of ever-present ingrained habits.

To break free from the shackles of my past and forge a new path forward, I consciously decided to step away from the time-traveling vehicle of my mind and into the future of my creation. I began by putting one foot in front of the other, embarking on a physical and mental renewal journey through walking. As I traversed the winding paths of nature, I found solace in the words of motivational speakers such as Les Brown, Jim Rohn, and Tony Robbins, whose voices served as inspiration in the darkness.

Yet, it was amidst the serene beauty of Mother Nature that I found true refuge from the tumult of my thoughts. Each weekend, without fail, I sought out the tranquility of parks and conservation areas, immersing myself in the splendor of the natural world. Amidst the rustling leaves and soaring branches, I found myself transported to a realm of timeless serenity, where the worries of yesterday and the fears of tomorrow held no sway. I know to some this may sound like "tree-hugging", but it works. It allows us to get out of our heads.

In those moments of quiet contemplation in nature, my body responded to the silent sentinels of the forest—the majestic trees that witness the passage of time.

Immersing myself in nature became more than a leisurely activity—it became a profound spiritual experience, a journey of self-discovery that allowed me to connect with the essence of life itself. Instead of merely observing the natural world, I allowed myself to engage actively with my surroundings on a profoundly personal level.

I found simplicity in life's wonders, reveling in the beauty of the world around me. Whether picking up a stick and skimming it across the surface of a tranquil lake or marveling at the intricate details of a single leaf, I was a carefree boy once again. I had the power to be reunited with my father and my lost brother during a time when I found joy in the sheer simplicity of existence. Each moment became a meditation, a reminder of the profound beauty in the smallest of things.

In nature's embrace, I was drawn to the boundless energy and vitality of another faithful companion, my dog Michonne. Dana rescued her at a tender eight months while our dearest Sammy was undergoing a cancerous tumor in his mouth. The cancer eventually prevented him from eating, and I was forced to bid farewell to the creature that ultimately saved my life. I wasn't prepared to love another dog, but Michonne was steadfast and patient, waiting for me to regain the ability to accept her into my heart. As I watched her frolic in the open fields, her infectious enthusiasm reminded me of the importance of living in the present moment. With each playful leap and joyous bark, she demonstrates the power of embracing life with open arms, free from the burdens of past regrets or future anxieties.

Through the practice of presence, I discovered a newfound appreciation for the blessings that surrounded me. It was an opportunity to reflect on the abundance of positivity in my life, a reminder that amidst the chaos and uncertainty of the world, there is still much to be grateful for. By remaining fully present, I found a sense of focus and clarity that allowed me to navigate life's challenges with grace and resilience.

Ultimately, I came to understand that while I may not have control over the events of the past or the uncertainties of the future, I have the power to shape my experience of the present moment. I realize now that life is a fleeting and precious gift and tomorrow is never promised.

You May be Right I may be Crazy

As a high school student navigating the corridors of adolescence, KISS 105 FM served as my music lifeline, through which the anthems of the eighties flowed freely into my soul. With his masterful storytelling, Billy Joel emerged as a beacon of inspiration, his lyrics weaving tales of love, loss, and the human condition.

Even now, as I traverse the highways of life, my trusty playlist serves as a timeless companion, a reminder of simpler times and enduring melodies. When Billy Joel's unmistakable chords fill the air, I can't help but surrender to the infectious rhythm, belting out the lyrics with reckless abandon, much to the amusement of onlookers at neighboring stoplights.

Beyond the realm of music lies another avenue of comfort, where words wield transformative power—the realm of writing. Writing is cathartic, an act of liberation, and a means of unburdening the soul and charting a path toward healing.

In my journal pages, I find sanctuary, a haven where raw and honest thoughts find refuge in dealing with the political climate and the culture wars. Transcribing my innermost thoughts onto paper allows me to move forward and make room for what is next.

Writing becomes my anchor, tethering me to the present moment and offering a break from my mind's ceaseless churning. It is a tool of empowerment, a catalyst for change. With each stroke of the pen, I confront my trauma head-on, refusing to allow the specters of the past to dictate my present. I unearth buried emotions, confront deep-seated fears, and emerge stronger and more resilient than before.

Through writing, I transform pain into purpose and sorrow into strength. It is a journey of self-reclamation, a testament to the indomitable power of the human spirit to transcend adversity and emerge victorious.

As I exit the field of law enforcement, I carry with me the lessons of the past and the promise of the future. Armed with the pen as my sword and the paper as my shield, I am a warrior of words… a champion of resilience, and it is my sincere hope that my story of survival helps you with yours.

Gratitude

As you dive into these pages, I extend my gratitude to you, the worthy reader somehow drawn to my story. Gratitude, a word often uttered but rarely appreciated, has been a cornerstone of my journey. It's not just about saying thanks; it's about cultivating a deep appreciation for the blessings in our lives, no matter the storms we weather.

In exploring gratitude, I've found comfort during my darkest hours. When the weight of the world threatened to crush me, and the echoes of loss reverberated through my soul, gratitude became my lifeline. It was a lifeline extended to me, even in the face of senseless violence that claimed the lives of many fellow deputies.

The scourge of the Covid pandemic cast a long shadow over our profession, claiming the lives of more law enforcement officers in 2020 than those who fell in the line of duty. Though transversing through chaos and uncertainty, gratitude emerged as my guide. Guiding me through the storm. It reminded me to cherish each moment, each breath, despite the pain and loss surrounding me.

But gratitude is not just a salve for our collective wounds; it's also a tool for personal growth and resilience. The pandemic forced many of us to confront our inner demons, sit with ourselves in silence, and reckon with our fears and insecurities. This reflective time was (and still is) a daunting era for law enforcement officers accustomed to the job's relentless demands.

Yet, gratitude reveals its true power in these moments of solitude. It reminds us to find beauty amid chaos and joy in the smallest victories. Gratitude allows us to embrace our humanity, acknowledge our vulnerabilities, and find strength in our shared experiences.

As the death toll climbed and the specter of fear loomed large, I turned my gaze inward, taking stock of the abundance that filled my life. In the quiet moments between the chaos, I was drawn to the simple pleasures that often go unnoticed. I found comfort in the loving embrace of my wife, whose constant support anchors me, and in my other faithful companion, Michonne, whose boundless affection reminded me of the power of unconditional love.

Gratitude is now my enduring lifeline. As a retired law enforcement officer and the spouse of a former teacher, I navigated the pandemic from a unique vantage point. While the world outside teetered on the brink of collapse, our jobs remained a steadfast anchor in the storm. It was a reminder of the resilience of the human spirit, a testament to the power of gratitude in the face of adversity.

Know Thyself

As I dove into self-discovery, one of my most trusted companions became self-awareness. During a routine walk, with the wisdom of Tony Robbins echoing in my ears, I stumbled upon a profound realization.

Robbins recounted a tale from his own life, a story of racing cars and navigating treacherous tracks. His instructor's words struck a chord within me: "Look not where you are headed, but where you want to go." At that moment, it was as if a floodgate had opened, inundating me with questions about my trajectory.

Like Robbins before his revelation, was I fixated on the obstacles in my path, careening toward them with reckless abandon? Or was I, perhaps, focused on a different destination altogether—a destination of hope, healing, and humanity?

In law enforcement, it's all too easy to become trapped in the trappings of the job, to view each encounter through the narrow lens of problem-solving. But what if, instead of fixating solely on the problem, we dared to see the person behind it? What if we approached each situation with a sense of empathy, a willingness to understand the human being at its core?

This shift in perspective marked a pivotal moment in my journey. It reminded me that actual change begins not with eradicating problems but with cultivating compassion in response to them. It was a call to action, a summons to look beyond the surface and seek out the humanity in every interaction.

Self-awareness is akin to possessing a power reminiscent of Neo's in the Matrix. It's the ability to manipulate my reality, a skill that may sound unconventional, but bear with me. In the intricate dance of life, our experience of reality is profoundly influenced by our reactions. By diligently tuning into my emotions and scrutinizing my reactions, I've found that events seem to unfold slowly as I navigate the labyrinth of decision-making.

Self-awareness has become my stalwart companion, like that trusted friend who watches out for your well-being. Picture the friend who discreetly informs you about a dangling piece of spinach in your teeth, sparing you from unwittingly parading it around all day. This friend lends a helping hand when a storm damages your roof, assisting in patching up the holes. They are the beacon of support, always ready to help whenever needed. Importantly, they're the voice of reason that prevents you from descending into the intricate mazes of political rabbit holes.

In my journey, the amalgamation of self-awareness and empathy has been transformative. It's not just about understanding myself; it's about extending that understanding to others. This synergy has made me a better man and a more adept and compassionate officer.

This revelation didn't occur overnight. It was a gradual process of self-discovery, a journey through the peaks and valleys of my emotional landscape. With each stride, I realized that this unique power of self-awareness, much like Neo's mastery of the Matrix, can be harnessed to reshape my reality and those around me. It's a potent tool that empowers me to navigate the complexities of my profession with newfound wisdom and resilience.

Chapter Nine

Scars

As I stand at the door of retirement, I'm confronted with the scars I obtained through the trials and tribulations of this profession. These scars, rather than festering wounds of resentment, represent my resilience. Though not visible to the naked eye, I've realized that emotional scars demand acknowledgment. They are not badges of honor to be flaunted, but they command a solemn reverence from within.

Each encounter with the grim realities of humanity, from murders to rapes, from child abuse to suicides, left its indelible mark upon my soul. The suicides, in particular, serve as reminders of personal tragedy, echoing the haunting memory of my brother's death. Beyond the blaring sirens and the peaceful removal of lifeless bodies, I'm acutely aware of the chasm left behind in the lives of the family; families left with unanswered questions and inconsolable grief.

The scars run deeper still when confronted with the shattered innocence of children, their eyes betraying a profound loss of innocence that rends the heart asunder. Amidst the cacophony of political discord and the relentless onslaught of the COVID-19 pandemic, the law enforcement family, like many others, grappled with loss. Officers who stood shoulder to shoulder one day were inexplicably absent the next, leaving behind a trail of scars that bore witness to their absence.

Yet, these scars, far from harbingers of destruction, serve as beacons of resilience. They implore me to stand steadfast in my commitment to those whose lives have been ravaged by adversity. They remind me of my 'why', the driving force behind my unwavering dedication to serve and protect. With each scar, I forge more profoundly into my self-awareness, compassion, and empathy, harnessing the collective weight of my experiences to overcome any obstacles in my path.

Throughout my adversity and despair, I took solace in the enduring legacy of these scars. They are not scars of defeat but of triumph, testaments to my unyielding resolve to rise above the shadows cast by adversity and emerge stronger, wiser, and more compassionate in their wake.

To Be Continued

On the auspicious day of August 9th, 2023, I bid farewell to my illustrious career in law enforcement, yet my journey of service to humanity shall persist. As the curtains close on this chapter of my life, I offer you this bit of advice, my brothers and sisters, in public safety: depart when you've amassed enough, not when you've endured enough. Too often, embittered souls exit this noble profession, proclaiming, "I've had enough!" It is much more gratifying to gaze into the looking glass and declare, "I have enough." Enough is not merely in material wealth but in the fulfillment derived from giving and receiving within our communities.

The law enforcement profession is unlike any other, where individuals willingly lay down their lives for strangers, and split-second decisions hold the power of life and death. It is an occupation that exacts a toll more significant than it bestows if one fails to tread cautiously. Yet, through the arduous journey, if one tends to one's well-being along the path, one can not only survive in their career but make it one in which they thrive.

As for me, I have conquered the demons that once haunted me. While they may occasionally linger at the periphery of my consciousness, they swiftly dissipate into oblivion. Demons, you see, are discerning creatures; they recognize when they are unwelcome and shun an audience's absence. Through the arsenal of self-awareness, self-confidence, and self-love, I have fortified my mind and erected an impregnable fortress where demons find no sanctuary.

So, as I bid farewell to the badge and uniform that adorned my persona for decades, I carry forth the invaluable lessons gleaned from the trenches of law enforcement. With unwavering resolve and a heart brimming with compassion, I embark on the next chapter of my odyssey, a journey illuminated by the light of self-discovery and redemption.

Final Thoughts

In the dimly lit room, amidst the silence broken only by the occasional beep of medical equipment, I sit, pen in hand, reflecting on the journey that led me here. As I delve into the pages of my story, I'm haunted by the memories that flicker in my mind like ghosts in the night.

It's easy to feel like there's nothing left to hold on to in this job. The weight of responsibility bears down heavily, and each day brings new challenges and uncertainties. I've seen families torn apart and relationships crumble under the immense strain of this profession. The toll it takes on our souls is immeasurable.

But amidst the darkness, some moments shine like beacons of hope—moments when I've touched countless lives in profound and understated ways. I remember a particular person I transported to jail, their eyes filled with anger and despair. They wanted to hurt someone, but at that moment, I became a lifeline. I intervened, and in doing so, perhaps I saved not only their life but the lives of others.

Then there are the medical calls, the ones that remind me of the fragility of life. I recall the time when EMS was still on its way, and I found myself performing CPR on an elderly man, my hands pressing down with a desperate urgency. I held them together in those critical moments, willing them to hang on until help arrived. And they did. I was part of saving another human.

I carry these moments with me every time I step out into the world. They act as fuel that propels me forward and are why I continue to serve despite the darkness that threatens to consume me. It's not just something I hear in the voice inside my head; it's a truth that resonates deep within me.

I have something to live for because I make a difference every day I step into the fray. It may be a small ripple in the vast ocean of chaos, but it's a ripple nonetheless. And that's enough to have kept me going in a world that often feels devoid of hope.

But beneath the surface, a little pain lingers—a pain all too familiar to those of us in this profession. It's a pain born from the trauma we witness, the burdens we carry, and the sacrifices we make. It's a pain often ignored, dismissed, or buried beneath layers of stoicism.

As a certified emotional intelligence trainer, I've made it my mission to bridge the gap between law enforcement and the community. For the past seven years, I've dedicated myself to helping officers understand the importance of acknowledging their trauma and learning to control their emotions in the face of adversity.

My story is one of pain and passion, of heartache and resilience. It speaks to the struggles we face as law enforcement officers and the profound impact we can have on the lives of those we serve. But it's also a story of hope—a reminder that even in our darkest moments, we can find light if only we're willing to look for it.

In the shadows of my agency, amidst the echoes of sirens and distant voices, I reflect on a moment that has stayed with me through the darkest times. It's a memory that cuts through the noise of trauma and pain, reminding me of the impact we can have, even in chaos.

As I sift through the files on my desk, each one a testament to the brokenness of our world, I'm transported back to a time when a glimmer of hope pierced the darkness. It was a day like any other, filled with the weight of responsibility and the relentless tide of despair. Yet amidst it all, there was a moment of clarity, a reminder of why I chose this path in the first place.

I remember the little girl's eyes wide with innocence and longing as she approached me with a simple yet profound declaration. "I wish you were my daddy," she said, her words carrying a weight far more remarkable than her years. At that moment, I knew that my presence and actions had made a difference in her life. It was a small victory in a sea of challenges, but it was enough to sustain me in the following days.

And then there was the young man, barely seventeen yet already hardened by the harsh realities of life. He approached me with a guarded expression, his distrust of authority evident in every word he spoke. "I don't usually like cops," he said, his tone hesitant yet sincere, "but you're okay." It was a simple statement that spoke volumes about the impact we can have when we choose empathy over indifference.

In these moments, I find solace among the chaos, a reminder of the good within us all. It's easy to become overwhelmed by the trauma we witness and to lose sight of the moments of triumph that lie beneath the surface. But as a certified emotional intelligence trainer, I've learned the importance of grounding ourselves in these moments and of recognizing our value even in the face of adversity.

For the past seven years, I've dedicated myself to bridging the gap between law enforcement and the community, helping officers understand the importance of acknowledging their trauma and controlling their emotions in the line of duty. It's a journey fraught with challenges and obstacles but worth taking.

Throughout my career in law enforcement, I've repeatedly stepped in when others needed help the most. It's become my defining purpose, my reason for being. Yet, within the weight of trauma and heartache that often accompanies this line of work, it's easy to lose sight of that purpose. Deep down, it's always there, driving me forward.

Let me take you on a journey through my experiences, where the shadows of the past sometimes clouded my vision but where I found my purpose again by embracing the moments that defined me and revisiting my "why."

Seven years ago, I embarked on a mission to bridge the gap between law enforcement officers and the communities they serve. As a certified emotional intelligence trainer, I've dedicated myself to helping officers understand the impact of trauma and emotional resilience, not just for their well-being but also for the betterment of the communities they protect and serve.

But this journey hasn't been easy. It's been filled with moments that tested my resolve and brought me face-to-face with the harsh realities of trauma in law enforcement.

I remember the first time I encountered a fellow officer struggling with the weight of the job. His eyes, once filled with determination, now carried a heavy burden of pain and exhaustion. It was a stark reminder of the toll this profession can take on a person's mental and emotional well-being.

Then there were the countless encounters with community members, each with their own stories of trauma and hardship. In those moments, I realized the importance of empathy and understanding, not just as a law enforcement officer but as a human being.

But there were moments of triumph and joy across the pain and struggles. For example, I witnessed fellow officers break down the barriers of mistrust and misunderstanding between law enforcement and the community through open dialogue and genuine empathy.

Or the countless times when I witness officers embrace their vulnerability and seek help for their mental health, breaking the stigma that surrounds mental illness in law enforcement.

These moments, both heart-wrenching and uplifting, have shaped my journey and reaffirmed my purpose. They've shown me that even in the darkest times, there's a reason to live and a purpose to fulfill.

So, to my fellow law enforcement officers and those we serve, including our families, I want you to know that you're not alone in your struggles. There are tools and support systems out there to help you navigate through the darkness and rediscover your purpose.

It's never too late to seek help, to address the trauma that comes with this profession, and to find healing and hope. Together, we can break down the barriers that divide us and build a stronger, more resilient community.

Tools for Coping with Trauma

Through my personal journey, I've unearthed a collection of indispensable tools crucial for navigating trauma. These tools have not only aided me in reclaiming and safeguarding my mental and emotional well-being but are poised to do the same for you.

Therapy

When the burden becomes overwhelming, seeking guidance from a therapist becomes a crucial lifeline. However, the choice of therapist holds immense significance, possibly ranking among the most pivotal decisions in one's life. Opting for a therapist experienced in assisting individuals within Public Safety is paramount. Their familiarity with our profession ensures a level of comprehension of our unique challenges.

To ascertain the suitability of a therapist, one must not shy away from posing pertinent questions:

- Inquire about their history of providing therapy to those in Public Safety.
- Assess their tenure in the field, aiming to gauge their understanding of our profession and its intrinsic motivations.
- Ensure their counsel aligns with your best interests, particularly regarding understanding the nuances of your job, rather than merely suggesting detachment from it.
- Probe about their experience with law enforcement officers to gauge their capacity to empathize and offer relevant support.
- Present hypothetical scenarios, such as thoughts of self-harm, to gauge their response and gauge their suitability for addressing sensitive issues.

- Express concerns regarding identity struggles, such as feeling confined to the role of a law enforcement officer, and evaluate their approach towards assisting in such matters.

By engaging in such dialogue, one can gauge the therapist's alignment with their needs and discern their ability to offer meaningful assistance in navigating the complexities of a career in law enforcement.

Employee Assistance Program

Another avenue worth considering is your EAP (Employee Assistance Program), which offers a secure environment conducive to your well-being. Often, individuals hesitate to avail themselves of agency resources, fearing repercussions, particularly concerning confidentiality breaches. However, it's essential to understand that legal safeguards exist to protect your privacy. Your agency cannot intrude into your therapy sessions; regulations are in place to ensure this. Thus, don't let apprehensions hinder you from accessing the support and assistance available through your EAP.

Go Green

To "Go Green" as a method of coping with trauma doesn't refer to environmental actions, as the phrase might suggest. Instead, it's a concept related to self-soothing and finding solace in nature. This approach involves spending time outdoors, particularly in green spaces like parks, forests, or gardens, to heal and restore emotional well-being.

Engaging with nature has been linked to various mental health benefits, including reduced stress levels, improved mood, and enhanced overall well-being. Natural environments' calming effects can provide a sense of peace and perspective, which can be particularly valuable for individuals dealing with trauma.

In essence, "Going Green" in the context of coping with trauma involves seeking refuge and renewal in natural settings, utilizing the restorative power of nature to support emotional healing and resilience.

Practice Self-Care

Self-care commences with prioritizing physical health, a foundation often overlooked. Begin with a daily practice of walking, a simple yet potent ritual. As you engage in this activity, your body releases dopamine, the neurotransmitter associated with pleasure and reward. Moreover, walking serves to purge your system of cortisol, the notorious stress hormone. By integrating this routine into your daily life, you actively mitigate the effects of stress while fostering a healthier mind and body.

Meditation

Ensuring I allocate time for meditation has become a cornerstone of my daily routine. Reflecting a decade ago, the idea of meditation might have elicited a chuckle from me, yet now, I recognize its profound importance. Quieting the mind is essential. It's imperative not to inundate oneself with negativity first thing in the morning, whether through the news or radio. Despite our brain's inclination toward negativity, we retain control over what we feed it. Creating a tranquil space for introspection sets the tone for the day, offering a serene foundation upon which to build our mental fortitude.

Practice Positive Self Talk

In navigating my daily challenges, I've integrated a practice of self-dialogue to maintain emotional balance. It's about reaffirming that I can steer my day toward positivity despite the hurdles. For instance, when confronted with angry individuals expressing grievances about a deputy, I consciously remind myself that their frustration is directed toward the circumstances, not me personally.

Crucially, I've cultivated a mindset that allows me to separate my emotions from those of others, recognizing that their reactions stem from their perceptions and experiences. This mental separation has been transformative, enabling me to avoid internalizing negativity and instead view situations objectively.

Embracing this perspective shift aligns with Wayne Dyer's wisdom: "When you change the way you look at things, the things you look at change." This principle underscores the power of perception in shaping our experiences. I preserve my emotional well-being and remain resilient in adversity by refusing to take personal offense or internalize unwarranted criticism.

In law enforcement, where authority often intersects with conflict, it's imperative to detach oneself from external judgments and maintain a clear sense of self. Rather than succumbing to reactionary responses or taking offense at perceived slights, I prioritize understanding and detachment, recognizing that others' opinions or actions do not define my worth.

Practice Self-Awareness

In my discussions with organizations, I emphasize the necessity of fighting darkness while ensuring it does not consume us in return. This principle resonates deeply with me, constantly reminding me to maintain vigilance over my well-being. This vigilance proves invaluable, particularly in high-stress scenarios such as confrontational traffic stops, where composure is paramount.

I refrain from hastily labeling such confrontations as rooted in racism, recognizing instead the importance of self-awareness in understanding human behavior. This commitment to self-awareness permeates every aspect of my daily life, guiding my actions and words on and off duty. Upon returning home from a taxing day, I undertake breathing exercises to release the tension accumulated during lengthy shifts. This practice, supported by scientific evidence, helps alleviate the physical and mental strain inherent in law enforcement duties.

Additionally, I draw upon lessons from past experiences, such as my time visiting Việtnam, to inform my actions. Removing my shoes upon entering my home serves as a symbolic gesture, reminding me to leave the stress and negativity of the outside world behind. These small rituals underscore the importance of maintaining boundaries between professional responsibilities and personal well-being, fostering a sense of balance and resilience in the face of adversity.

Get From Behind the Badge

In our line of duty, it's easy to become consumed by our role, losing sight of the multifaceted individuals we genuinely are. Beyond the badge lies a wealth of passions, interests, and talents waiting to be rediscovered. To break free from the all-encompassing identity of law enforcement, it's crucial to venture beyond our comfort zones.

Consider engaging in volunteer work or activities that challenge you. Stepping into unfamiliar territory allows us to see ourselves as officers and fellow humans capable of making meaningful connections beyond our professional roles. For instance, volunteering at a school offers a unique opportunity to interact with children non-authoritatively. By shedding the uniform and simply being ourselves, we can forge genuine connections based on shared humanity rather than perceived roles.

Embracing discomfort and exploring diverse experiences is essential in reconnecting with our true selves. By venturing into unfamiliar territories, engaging in hobbies, and traveling, we open ourselves up to new perspectives and possibilities. Ultimately, prioritizing our humanity over our professional identity enables us to become better officers and individuals, enriching our personal and professional lives.

Cultivate Gratitude

Nurture a sense of gratitude by immersing yourself in experiences that illuminate the blessings in your life, anchoring you firmly in the present.

Pen Down Your Story

To truly navigate the complexities of our profession, one must delve deep within themselves, regardless of external circumstances. We must craft our narrative as the authors of our stories. Witnessing law enforcement officers nationwide allowing external voices to define their identities and missions is disheartening. We cannot afford to relinquish control of our narratives, allowing others to dictate who we are and why we chose this path.

Remember, the decision to pursue a career in law enforcement was driven by a desire to serve, protect, and positively impact society. Despite our challenges and criticisms, we must remain steadfast in our commitment to these values. I've experienced pressure to conform to external perceptions, even within my agency. Despite the support of our community, the influence of outside voices can still weigh heavily on our minds.

However, it's essential to recognize that external validation does not define our worth and purpose. We possess an internal compass honed through training and experience, guiding us towards what is right and just. Our actions, driven by this moral compass, inherently bring value to the lives of those we serve.

Therefore, I implore you to take ownership of your story. Do not allow external forces to dictate your narrative or lead you astray from your passions. Trust in your convictions, uphold your values, and continue to make a difference in the lives of others. Ultimately, the power to shape our destinies lies within us.

2nd Alarm Project
https://2ndalarmproject.org/?gclid=CjwKCAjwseSoBhBXEiwA9iZtxsNjx4dGdVP1k_grMCFey2O3LEErNedtDvy0JT60FSkcSBpF_WkFfRoCRREQAvD_BwE

https://ucfrestores.com/

UCF RESTORES provides its evidence-based clinical treatment services to individuals experiencing PTSD and other trauma-related concerns

https://helpforourheroes.com/police-officers-and-mental-health/

Individual and Group Therapy

About The Author

Author, Speaker, and Retired Lieutenant, Fred Jones has worked in various roles over his 25+ year career in Public Safety -- concluding his career as a Lieutenant in Professional Standards and as a Public Information Officer at his agency. Based in Lake County, Florida, he has served his community in the capacity of a Detective, Patrol Deputy, Patrol Supervisor, Correctional Officer, and School Resource Deputy. But his quest to bridge the gap between community and law enforcement has been his most passionate pursuit.

Throughout his career, his goal has always been to help citizens understand the human behind the badge -- and to help those behind the badge understand the citizens they serve.

An advocate for Officer Wellness, he is a nationally certified Emotional Intelligence trainer, De-escalation Specialist, and Subject Matter Expert.

Today, Lieutenant Jones (continues to serve as a liaison between the community and law enforcement and has been recognized on a local and national level for his contributions. In addition to being a motivational speaker and instructor who has spoken at TEDx, various conferences, and schools throughout the U.S., he is a Crisis Intervention Training instructor, which is a nationally recognized de-escalation course.

Lieutenant Jones is a graduate of Flagler College with a Bachelor of Science in Public Administration and a Master of Science in Criminal Justice from Columbia College. He resides in Thailand with his wife, Dana, and his dog Michonne. He spends his time volunteering at schools and orphanages and documents his journey in Thailand on his YouTube channel Far Away Fred

For more info, or to invite Fred Jones to speak at your event,

visit www.FredJonesSpeaks.net

Made in the USA
Columbia, SC
23 July 2024

38846094R00083